HOW TO
GET FAT

THE *Self-Hurt* SERIES

**KNOCK
KNOCK**™
VENICE, CALIFORNIA

Published by
Knock Knock
1633 Electric Avenue
Venice, CA 90291
www.knockknock.biz

Illustrated by Mark Weber

This book is a work of humor meant solely for entertainment purposes. It is
not intended to recommend or advise regarding the prevention, diagnosis,
or treatment of any medical condition. The advice contained in this book is
intended as a parody of diet books; actually following the advice contained
herein may be harmful to your health. In no event will Knock Knock be liable
to any reader for any damages, including direct, indirect, incidental, special,
consequential, or punitive damages, arising out of or in connection with the
use of the information contained in this book. So there.

ISBN: 978-160106039-6
UPC: 8-25703-50101-8

CONTENTS

CHAPTER 1 7

Introduction:
It's Time to Get Fat

CHAPTER 2 25

Changing Your Fat-itude:
Getting into the Mindset

CHAPTER 3 47

"But I'm Small-Boned!"
Overcoming Excuses and Obstacles

CHAPTER 4 65

Determining Food Intake:
Setting Yourself Up to Succeed

CHAPTER 5 81

What to Eat:
Developing the Right Habits

CHAPTER 6..99

Vittles Galore:
Buying the Right Foods

CHAPTER 7..121

How to Eat:
Making the Most of Your Instincts

CHAPTER 8..143

Where to Eat:
Setting the Stage for Weight Gain

CHAPTER 9..163

Cease All Exercise:
The Sedentary Life

CHAPTER 10..179

Conclusion:
Taking Fat to the Next Level

CHAPTER 1
INTRODUCTION: IT'S TIME TO GET FAT

THIS BOOK WILL GET YOU FAT.
With all the opportunities not to eat, all the motivations to exercise to excess, it isn't easy to pack on the pork. But now there's help. With this book, you'll learn how to change your attitude, overcome obstacles, and foster a food-friendly lifestyle. Full of tips, tools, and strategies for successful weight gain, *How to Get Fat* will add pounds to your body and keep them there. Like so many of us, you're probably fed up with the struggle to gain. No matter what shape or size you currently are, if you follow this simple plan, you'll get fat. Short of actually sticking this book in your

back pocket and stepping on the scale, you won't find an easier, more enjoyable way to achieve and maintain your desired overweight. Pat yourself on the back for making the commitment to a lifetime of obesity, then grab your knife and fork—it's time to get fat! You'll learn how to:

- Find the mental fat within.

- Determine your goal weight.

- Consume more calories with every snack, meal, and binge.

- Pass up fruits and vegetables in favor of fats, sugar, and carbs.

- Eat emotionally, celebrating joy and soothing pain.

- Set up your environment for complete food-friendliness.

- Avoid exercise at all costs.

So Many Reasons to Gain

Motivation is key to achieving any worthwhile goal. Before you can successfully
increase your body mass, you've got to *want*
to be fat. There are more reasons than ever
to make obesity your lifestyle choice, from
celebrating your inner self to pledging alle-
giance to the flag to enjoying better sex.

"You have such a great personality."

With the contemporary mainstream
view that slender is attractive, many
burdens fall upon the slim—they have
to spend time pumping and primping,

Words of Plenty

"When we lose 20 pounds, we may be losing the
20 best pounds we have! We may be losing the
pounds that contain our genius, our humanity, our
love and honesty."
—Woody Allen

---

fend off unwanted advances, worry whether people like them for who they really are. Once you're fat, however, you can extricate yourself entirely from the shallow, demeaning race for physical perfection and its spoils. The fastest and easiest way to avoid criticism, rejection, and disappointment is to take yourself out of the race. Once you're obese, you'll have the opportunity to base your self-worth entirely on your character and personality and then wait for others to notice. And when they do, you'll know it's for all the right reasons.

As American as Apple Pie à la Mode

The best at being the biggest, an estimated 30 percent of adults in the United States are considered obese,

while another 35 percent are overweight. Life, liberty, and the pursuit of
happiness include eating whatever we
want, whenever we want, then buying
bigger, stretchier clothes. For those of
us lucky enough to live in a bountiful,
convenience-oriented democracy, it's
important to take full advantage of
what we have; to decline makes light
of the poverty of less fortunate
nations. After all, isn't dieting while
others starve the height of selfish
cynicism? As Americans, we have the
right to choose a life of abundance and
leisure; indeed, it's one of the charac-
teristics that distinguishes the United
States as a world leader. For example,
imagine that you're traveling in Paris
and you stop in a quaint café for a
croissant. The waiter approaches and

speaks to you in English. How does he know you're American? Because you're fat! Represent your country with pride—if you're not careful, Canada will catch up.

Historical Precedents: Thin Wasn't Always In

We have the current misfortune to live during a cult of thin, but this hasn't always been the case. Fat used to be synonymous with wealth, privilege, and decadence. Women wore bustles to accentuate their derrières, creating the illusion of ample charms. Fertility has long been associated with fatness. The earliest known three-dimensional carving of a human being, the Venus of Willendorf—from 15,000 BCE, the very first supermodel—proudly displays large,

Chubby Lovin': BBW and BHM

Have you ever bemoaned the lack of special-ized ways to meet a potential significant other? Weight gain affords you entrée into an elite dating world. A quick Internet keyword search will yield a wealth of online dating websites patron-ized by like-minded and like-bodied singles. As with any unique culture, however, it's important to know the lingo before diving in:

BBW: Big Beautiful Woman

BHM: Big Handsome Man

SSBBW or SSBHM: Super-Size BBW or BHM

SA: Size Acceptance

Bear: Fat, hairy man

FA: Fat Admirer

FFA: Female Fat Admirer

HWP: Height/Weight Proportional

Chubby Chaser: Appreciator of fat

Unfortunately, when dating fat, it's still necessary to watch out for objectivization. In the case of fat fetishes, you are no more appreciated for who you are than emaciated cover models. Be particularly wary of "feeders," who derive sexual pleasure from encour-aging "feedees" to gain vast amounts of weight. While this would undoubtedly improve your girth, it could come at the expense of your self-esteem.

pendulous breasts and an enormous belly hanging over her lusciously plump thighs. No lesser beauty than Sophia Loren said, "Everything you see I owe to spaghetti." While images of slim, toned bodies dominate the media today, there are nonetheless plenty of pop culture contributors who sing the praises of fuller figures. Queen's "Fat-Bottomed Girls," Sir Mix-a-Lot's "Baby Got Back," and Spinal Tap's "Big Bottom" are only a few. Rap and hip-hop artists—already known for celebrating voluptuous ladies—have co-opted the word "fat" and changed it to "phat," a positive term that conveys power, strength, quality, and sex-appeal. As you become fat, just think about the fact that you're also becoming *phat*.

More Cushion for the Pushin'

According to a recent survey, only 40 to 45 percent of thin women say they enjoy sex, as contrasted with 85 percent of fat women. A whopping 70 percent of fat women assert that they almost always reach orgasm as opposed to 29 percent of slender women. Soft rolls of flesh are meant to envelop, to provide warmth, comfort, and pleasure. Soon there will be more of you to love, and as *you* get bigger, so will your orgasms.

Make 'Em Stare: Fat Gives You Presence

Because skinny people blend in, they need help distinguishing themselves. Just look at any advertisements for beauty products, clothing, and luxury items—they all proclaim that the goods will make the consumer stand out in a crowd. In a sea of basic bodies, apparently, an average-sized person requires makeup, wardrobe, and props to be noticed. Forget the fuss—just be fat. Not only will you get noticed, people will stare and make way for you. A heavy man can dominate any situation—Louis XIV used artificial padding to augment his already imposing physique. A Rubenesque woman pulls all eyes in her direction. By filling it with your own body, you'll own any space!

It's Good for You

With so many of us growing larger year after year, there are dire prognostications of a "global obesity epidemic." Increasingly, however, researchers are coming forward with

Large Lingo: Badonkadonk

Ample, voluptuous, and sexy rear end, especially when topped by a narrower waist and dramatic derrière cleavage. Onomatopoetic term for the perceived rhythmic sound such buttocks make while strutting their stuff. Similar to *junk in the trunk* and *bootylicious*.

studies that refute these alarmist claims. In 2005, the Centers for Disease Control revealed through their own studies that being extremely overweight is not nearly as lethal as previously claimed. Obesity has fallen from number 2 to number 7 in the leading causes of preventable death in the United States, landing behind car accidents and guns—and nobody's recommending that we stop driving. While studies are increasingly debunking the doomsday obesity predictions of the last decade, other data show that the real harm lies in *losing* weight: regaining pounds lost during yo-yo dieting (as 95 percent of dieters do) is profoundly more detrimental to your health than merely being—and staying—fat.

And It's So Much Fun

When it comes to getting fat, the journey is part of the reward. Once you're clear on why you want to gain, the next step is making it happen. A big new project can seem quite daunting, but you're in luck with this one: getting fat is almost as fun as *being* fat.

"Bad" Food Tastes Good

Whether sweet or savory, high-fat, calorie-rich food generally tastes better than its deprivation-driven counterparts. In this respect, you've got evolution on your side. Humans developed sweet tooths in order to choose the nonpoisonous sweet berries over the bitter toxic ones. When finding enough to eat was a challenge, our bodies learned to love rich, fatty meats. At its most basic, food is fuel, and now, for the aspiring fat person, it's also the gateway to being overweight. But don't ignore the fact that food can be so much more than that! You'll be able to liberate your inner gourmand and revel in the fat-inducing effects of rich, flavorful, decadent delights. They don't have to be fancy or expensive, just delicious. Whatever your particular yens and hankerings, you'll enjoy the food you'll be eating to get fat. What better motivation to overindulge than to focus on those foods you most love? In your path to fat, you'll not only be encouraged but *instructed* to eat as many and as much of the foods you crave.

Satisfying Your Oral Fixation

Even if taste isn't where you derive your pleasure, not to worry, because eating can satisfy in so many other ways. Do you smoke? Chew gum? Love to talk? As a child, did you suck your thumb? Like many people, you're probably orally fixated. The beauty of an oral fixation is that you can learn to channel happiness, anxieties, and boredom into eating. You'll be amazed how many needs eating

Moving to Mauritania

In Mauritania, a fat wife is so prized that families force-feed their daughters and send them to fattening farms in order to increase their attractiveness to a potential husband. In this North African country, the practice of "gavage" (the French word for fattening geese for foie gras) assures that wives will reflect on their husbands as symbols of wealth. If belly massage (to loosen the skin) and drinking 14 gallons of camel's milk doesn't do the trick, some women resort to dangerous hunger-inducing pills and steroids.

can fulfill, whether cathartic, celebratory, or meditative.

No Pain, All Gain

With your palate and your mind experiencing so much pleasure, your body also deserves a treat, and it's got a big one: your days of "feeling the burn" are over. From skipping the gym in the morning and sleeping an extra hour to canceling your trainer in favor of lunch with friends, the focus on fat will give you the opportunity to relax. If you don't feel like doing anything, you won't, because laziness, lethargy, and, above all, television-watching will yield top results in your new quest (see chapter 9, "Cease All Exercise: The Sedentary Life").

A World of Fulfillment in Fat

You're about to experience one of the most enriching processes of your life. You don't want to gain in the short-term only to lose again—you want to make the pounds stick. For lasting change, you'll create a fat-promoting lifestyle by shifting your mentality, overcoming challenges, and discovering untold stores of inner strength and resilience.

Over the coming weeks and months, you'll be amazed at the changes you accomplish. Your clothes will grow tighter. You'll gain a double chin, and maybe even a triple. As the months pass, your friends will do a double-take when they see you. The day will come when you to request a seat belt extension on the airplane. Finally, your burgeoning rolls of glorious flesh will prevent you from seeing your toes. It's an endlessly exciting progression.

As you transition from plump to portly to fat, you'll discover that there's so much more to obesity than just additional flesh. If you've ever felt like something was missing from your life, *How to Get Fat* will help you fill that nameless, unsettling void with food. Once you've filled your belly, you'll know what it really means to be fulfilled.

CHAPTER 2
CHANGING YOUR FAT-ITUDE: GETTING INTO THE MINDSET

THE ROAD TO BULK BEGINS ABOVE
the neck. While getting fat is a physical
transformation, if you want succeed in
gaining weight—and keeping it on—the
real metamorphosis must take place in your
mind. Not only will a new attitude lead to
change in your body, it will ease the necessary but initially foreign lifestyle changes
you're about to undertake, speeding your
journey toward obesity. In this chapter,
we'll show you:

- How to develop a carpe diem
  approach to food.

- Why working from home is the

best choice for maintaining your
fat lifestyle.

- Why sleeping as little as possible
  will support your weight gain.

- How you can be pro-fat *and* proactive.

Life Is a Banquet

Food for the body is food for the soul.
Wouldn't you rather go through life feeling
that each day is special, important, and
worth living? A life fully experienced revels
in all that the senses have to offer. Your
outlook—as well as your girth—will come
to reflect the oversized joy and happiness in
which you partake.

Seize the Cake

When you see a luscious cake under
glass, you might be tempted to think,

"Oh, I could have cake like that any-time. Why bother now?" This per-spective is patently false. No two delicacies are exactly alike—those you encounter on any given day, in any given restaurant, grocery store, or kitchen, are unlike any you've experienced before, and you'll *never* have the chance to try them again. Different chefs, varying ingredients, disparate techniques, and even fluc-tuating humidity levels and time left out in the open air will yield subtle nuances you can't even imagine. If you pass that cake by, you'll never know whether it could have been the best combination of layers and frost-ing you'd ever tasted.

Not only does this live-in-the-moment philosophy encompass special occasions (pumpkin pie at Thanksgiving, Grandma's brisket, anything eaten while traveling), it also extends to everyday staples. While it's true that your favorite store-brand cookies always taste the same, the *circumstances* surrounding their consumption will differ. A birthday party, a girls' night out, an evening of television—food is essential to the mix.

Before and After

Ramp up your motivation by taking "before" and "after" pictures of yourself. Initially you'll find it difficult to look at snapshots of your "before" skinny body, as your sharp collarbones and flat stomach may repulse you. Don't despair! Soon your six-pack will recede behind a curtain of sumptuous fat. With time, the only way you'll know you have bones at all with an x-ray. Do yourself a favor and document your miraculous transformation. Pictures of your portly self will serve as a visual pat on the back for all your hard work.

Once you've allowed yourself to indulge in food, you'll realize that your newfound lust for life extends into other arenas. If, as many of us have, you've tried for years to get fat, don't let the fact that you haven't yet attained your goal weight get in the way of living your life to the fullest. All too often, fat-seekers put off life's pleasures because they worry they aren't heavy enough to deserve them. Rather than saying "I'll go on that cruise when I reach 250 pounds," by eating in the moment, you'll find that you stop putting your life on hold.

It's time to stop hiding behind your thinness. Deprivation in any other arena is just as damaging as deprivation in your diet. You have a greater chance of success in your weight gain when you're experiencing joy and fun in your life. If you delay making your dreams come true, you'll delay your dreams of fatness. When you have doubts, repeat the weight-gain mantra: always indulge, never deny.

The More of You the Merrier

It makes sense that laugh lines communicate how much mirth a person has experienced, and the same applies to rolls of fat—they demonstrate all their owner's fun times. Girth is a highly visible pleasure-meter. Evidence of lifelong denial is nothing to celebrate—who wants to die a reed-thin, face-lifted, pickled facsimile of a human being? The iconic image of the "jolly" fat person didn't happen by accident. Get fat and show others how much more you've relished life. Your body is your proof that you went to the party and outlasted everybody else.

You Deserve It

You're worthy of every morsel you put into your mouth. Because you appreciate the bounty of scent, texture, and taste, it's your right to take that last piece of torte from some self-denier who will actually feel guilty eating it. You understand the satisfaction to be found in food and drink, and because you're in the know, you deserve a higher level of enjoyment.

Supporting Your Quest for Fat

While it's possible to get fat by changing only your food consumption, if elements of your lifestyle are working against you, it will only be that much harder. A few small changes in your habits and environment will make a world of difference in maintaining your get-fat mindset.

No Professional Physical Activity

If your job involves manual labor—construction, mail delivery, or professional sports—your career is standing in the way of a fatter you. One approach is to do what you can to limit walking, lifting, and moving at work; if you're truly committed to gaining weight and keeping it on, however, you'll want to consider a career change. For gaining weight, sedentary is the way to go: get a desk job and just watch the pounds creep on. While many people won't have

> ## Large Lingo: Muffin Top
>
> The adorable bubble of flesh that blossoms over the waistband of pants; named for the tastiest part of the breakfast pastry.

this option, the best way to gain the most weight is to work from home, where you not only have complete control over your inactivity, letting whole days pass without taking more than a few steps, you can more easily multi-task by eating while you work.

Sleep: Obesity's Enemy

Research has shown a link between obesity and lack of sleep. The sleep-deprived show higher levels of two hormones that increase appetite, and they may retain fat more rigorously than the well-rested. Additionally, the longer you stay awake, the more time you'll have to eat—enough for a fourth or even fifth meal. The optimum weight-gaining sleep level is four to five hours per night, but studies show that even fifteen minutes less sleep than necessary will pack on the pounds.

Television: Friend of Fat

Television will prove one of your best weight-gain tools. It's sedentary, it's the perfect accompaniment to mindless snacking, and it's entertaining. The commercials will trigger cravings you didn't know you had. Or, if you're not game for the ads, get a digital recorder and speed through them—but remember to put the program on pause so you can head to the kitchen for refills.

Medicate While Self-Medicating

Many antidepressants will cure your blues *and* augment the rolls on your belly. If you're not currently undergoing treatment for depression, anxiety, or other psychological impairments, take a moment to assess the state of your mental health. Could you use a little pick-me-up? Talk to your doctor about medications that might help your emotional well-being as well as add a little something extra to your waistline.

Time to Quit Smoking

If you're a smoker, and you quit now, to coincide with your journey into weight gain, you'll get fat so easily it'll be like cheating. Some studies show that smokers can gain up to 10 pounds after kicking the habit—and that's

Movie Munching

Even though most actors are woefully slender, they nonetheless chow down on-screen. When you need a little inspiration to boost your caloric intake, draw on this group of films that celebrate food. Let your mouth water as you watch the characters prepare decadent feasts with love and passion. Allow your belly to rumble as the camera drifts over succulent ingredients, bubbling pots, and rising dough. Even try coordinating your dinner with the movie in advance to simulate the experience of enjoying a meal with your favorite actors!

9½ Weeks (1986)

Babette's Feast (1987)

Big Night (1996)

Chocolat (2000)

Eat Drink Man Woman (1994)

Like Water for Chocolate (1992)

Soul Food (1997)

Tampopo (1985)

Waitress (2007)

Willy Wonka and the Chocolate Factory (1971)

without trying. Researchers debate the reason for post-quitting weight gain, but one theory points to nicotine's role in increasing a smoker's metabolic rate. Upon quitting, your body is triggered to hoard fat. What's more, with your new commitment to cease all exercise, you'll add even more flab. A study published in the American Journal of Public Health revealed that former smokers who took up exercise only gained 4 pounds, while sedentary former smokers averaged an 8.5-pound increase. Of course, smoking is also bad for you, another reason to quit.

Advocate for Your Choice

Never underestimate the influence your social environment has on sustaining your new attitudes—in some ways, it takes a village to get you fat. The people who surround you can either help or hinder your dreams of obesity, so you'll want to determine who supports you and who can't get behind your goals. But it won't serve your purposes to complain about those who detract from your mission—it's up to you to make the world a fatter place.

Spread the Word

Whether you inform them one by one or throw yourself an "I'm getting fat" party, you'll want to tell everybody in your life of your commitment to gain weight. As you break the news, carefully gauge your friends' and family members' reactions. Those who are excited about your goal are keepers, especially the ones who want to indulge with you. Under their watchful eyes, you're more likely to stick to your eating routine, and they'll be excellent supports for you when fall off the wagon.

Be prepared for the fact that some members of your social circle may initially express disappointment. Remember, they're used to you the way you are, and your strength of commitment may scare them—and force them to take a look at their own unaddressed challenges. Perhaps they'll worry that your role in their lives will change, that you won't be their salad-bar buddy anymore, or you won't be available for morning runs. Reassure these friends that there are plenty of new activities for you to share. While your lifestyle is changing, your good friendship won't.

You'll want to be careful, however, to determine whether certain members of your circle are naysayers. You'll encounter two types of detractors: those who disagree with your particular goal of weight gain and those who don't want to see you succeed at any goal due to their own issues with self-loathing, lack of discipline, and jealousy. With the former, agree to disagree, and let them know that you'll need their support—or at least their silence—during the tender early stages of your personal change. As for the latter, drop them. They're toxic.

Find Fat Friends

No matter how supportive your civilian friends may be, there's nothing like sharing this experience with

someone who's on the same journey or someone who's already made
the trip. Other gainers will pitch in
with advice and tales of their own
fat growth, and you'll develop a community of like-minded friends. There
are so many ways to dive in, from the
National Association to Advance Fat
Acceptance (NAAFA) to dating sites
that specialize in fat lovers.

Objectify Thyself

In the last 10 years, plus-size modeling has
exploded in response to the fashion industry's
belated realization that the average (albeit seri-
ously underweight) size in the United States is a
14. With the burgeoning demand, new agencies
have opened and existing agencies have estab-
lished plus-size divisions, with models ranging
from sizes 12 to 20. How-to books and an entire
magazine, *Plus*, have dedicated themselves to
the art, and for those seeking hands-on tips, full-
figured modeling academies offer their services.

Let Corporate America Know You're Fat

Given the number of people who've made the decision to be fat, it's bad business that corporate America has ignored these consumers for so long (except, of course, in supplying the food). Those of us who've made the fat choice not only have a right to be heard, we have a right to be accommodated.

Instead of muttering to yourself about the size of airplane seats or the narrow aisles in supermarkets and restaurants, or silently fuming because your favorite designer doesn't make clothing in your size, you can do something about it. Write letters, blog, start a consumer website, and organize protests and boycotts. As you gain weight and your self-esteem improves, not only will your activism make the world a better place, it will, more importantly, give you a new-found sense of personal power.

Your voice can make a difference. Others have been speaking their minds to big business, and it's working. To accommodate the ever-growing American population, everything from car seats to coffins are getting bigger. Yielding to the reality of its growing customers, the Federal Aviation Administration (FAA) has increased the approved passenger weight by 10 pounds in order to ensure safety aboard flights. The plus-size clothing industry has burgeoned to $23 billion a year. Doctors now use longer needles when drawing blood in order to penetrate fatter layers of skin. And a chief reason for rebuilding Fenway Park was to fit today's Boston Red Sox fan—the seats are now 4 inches roomier. There's never been a better time to be fat.

Fat Mind, Fat Body

You're well on the road to turning any thin-minded thoughts around and reaching your goal weight that much more easily. It's natural, however, that at this early stage you still have some excuses for keeping the weight off. Not to worry—the next chapter will knock them down, one by one.

CHAPTER 3
"BUT I'M SMALL-BONED!"
OVERCOMING EXCUSES AND OBSTACLES

IF YOU STRUGGLED TO ACHIEVE obesity before, you probably have a host of convenient excuses for staying slim. While it's entirely understandable that you've hidden behind these thoughts, it's time now to stop relying on them. By deconstructing the most common reasons people cite for keeping their weight down, we'll show you how little water these excuses actually retain. Of course, we all have different bodies and come to the fat-seeking table with diverse life experiences, so there's no doubt that some people will have more obstacles than others. For some of you, your set of issues may require the extra support of a therapist. But for most, this chapter will reveal the many myths surrounding weight gain as well as teach you how to overcome any biological and social challenges you may face, including:

- What your ancestry can reveal about your ability to gain.

- How to outsmart a high metabolism.

- How to maximize your body's potential, whether your physical type is apple, pear, or banana.

- How to harness the many wonderful side effects of aging.

When analyzing and tackling your own excuses, just remember that everyone struggles with something. The plus-sized models you see in the Lands' End catalog didn't get that way overnight, and if you actually talked to them, they'd probably mention that they face many of the same challenges as you. The trick is to work with your own physique, heart, and mind to develop the right weight-gain program for you.

"My parents/family are thin!"

It's a tough pill to swallow, but some people are genetically predisposed to thinness. Your genetic makeup, however, doesn't have to stand in your way. If you inherit prematurely gray hair, you have the option to dye it. If your mom passed down her flat feet, you can get yourself fitted for orthotics. Everyone has inherited obstacles to overcome. In the realm of weight gain, you might have to work a little harder than an individual with a family history of obesity, but with dedication, you'll succeed, because there's something more powerful than genes: the laws of thermodynamics. If you consume more calories than you expend, you'll gain weight, no matter your family tree.

For some people, overcoming this challenge is simply a matter of looking beyond your slim parents and grandparents, whose physiques may have been more a result of under-eating than metabolism. People whose ancestors originate from areas with

Mirror, Mirror

Would you like to look into the future and the see the fatter you? Through the science of optics, it's not only possible, but easy. All it takes is a convex (bending outward) mirror to catch a glimpse of what awaits you at the end of your journey. Invest in a convex mirror and your image can serve as a daily reminder of your goal. This is the opposite of so-called "skinny mirrors" which distort their reflections with concavity (bending inward). Flip this self-destructive tactic around and get yourself a fat mirror so you can see yourself as a fatty as you become one!

historically irregular food supplies—like Africa, parts of Asia, the Americas, Eastern Europe, and the Pacific Islands—have a tendency to crave calorie-dense, high-fat foods and store weight in case of famine. Your legacy of familial weight gain doesn't have to be recent—if it's there, even a few generations back, you may have more genetic support for your weight gain than you thought.

"I've always been slender!"

Studies show that those who were skinny as a child or an adolescent are less likely to gain weight as adults. What the statistics don't show, however, is that plenty of people who were thin when young have gone on to great success in increasing their girth. Factors such as age and lifestyle choices can jump-start your fat cells—we'll show you how.

"My metabolism is too fast!"

While this excuse does hold for some unlucky people, for most of us, this justification is off-limits. Genes only contribute about 10 percent to the metabolism speed, whereas elements such as age, activity, diet, muscle-to-fat ratio, and hormones comprise the other determining 90 percent. For those who are genuinely cursed with a higher metabolic rate (burning calories at a faster pace), there are many ways to circumvent your metabolism and outsmart your body's natural tendency to be thin.

To combat a fast metabolism, it's highly effective to cease physical activity and lose muscle (see chapter 9, "Cease All Exercise: The Sedentary Life"). A sedentary 125-pound woman may burn fewer than 1,750 calories a day, while an overly active

125-pound woman can burn 2,200. That 450-calorie difference equals roughly nine Oreos. If you're sedentary *and* you eat the nine Oreos, that's like a 900-calorie gain!

In the quest to gain weight, continuous food consumption is encouraged. However, if you have a naturally high metabolism, you'll want to consider skipping meals here and there. Although you'll miss out on calories and fat, your body will go into starvation mode and hoard fuel. In the end, you'll have eaten less but gained more.

While a fast metabolism is indeed a sur- mountable obstacle to weight gain, there is some good news: the metabolism slows naturally with age. Women over 30, for example, can anticipate a decrease of 2 to 4 percent every 10 years.

"It's healthy to be skinny!"

There are so many health benefits to fat. First of all, it's all-natural; a fat body is an organic body. Beyond that, however, fat's contributions to wellness are endless. Dropping pounds rapidly, losing excessive weight, or being underweight can cause hair loss, cessation of menstruation and other fertility problems, a grumpy disposition, brittle bones and an increased likelihood of osteoporosis, and premature death. Medical interventions on weight such as liposuction and gastric-bypass procedures can cause grave injury and even death, but to become or stay fat, you will never need surgery. Diet pills have flooded the market over the years, all promising weight loss but often delivering debilitating and even deadly results. And if you're under 110 pounds, your health is shaky enough that you can aren't even allowed to donate blood.

Global Corpulence

While South Pacific countries are the most overweight in the world, and Kuwait just barely nudges out the United States for third place, if you factor in total population, the United States is the clear world leader in the race to gain. As a fat-seeker, you will of course want to live among those who embrace your values.

Most Desirable Countries		
Rate	Country	% Overweight
1	United States	74.1
2	Argentina	69.4
3	Egypt	69.4
4	Mexico	68.1
5	Australia	67.4
6	Chile	65.3
7	Venezuela	65.2
8	United Kingdom	63.8
9	Saudi Arabia	63.5
10	Canada	61.1

Least Desirable Countries		
Rate	Country	% Overweight
1	Eritrea	4.4
2	Ethiopia	5.6
3	Bangladesh	6.1
4	Vietnam	6.4
5	Sri Lanka	7.4
6	Nepal	8.4
7	Congo	9.1
8	Cambodia	11.3
9	Burundi	12.9
10	Zambia	13

Top overweight countries selected among those having populations of 10 million and above.
All percentages from Forbes.com, "World's Fattest Countries," February 28, 2007.

"I'm small-boned!"

Fortunately, this excuse is the easiest one to puncture. Do you really think that all the gloriously fat people whose bodies you covet have enormous skeletons underneath a thin layer of skin? It's true that some people are naturally smaller or larger than others, but bones have no effect on the ability to gain weight. You can be petite and fat, and you can be tall and fat. You can be a fat jockey or a fat rugby player. "Small-boned" is just a euphemism for a slender person who lacks the drive to get fat.

"I'm male!"

It's true—men and women put on weight differently. Not only do males have less body fat than females, an adult male has 10 to 20 percent more muscle than an adult female of the same age and size. Because muscle burns more energy than fat, a man's calorie requirements average 10 to 20 percent higher than a woman's. In general, women generate fat more easily and have a number of gains over men. The earlier a woman began menstruating, the heavier she will be as an adult. Mothers who hold onto 5 pounds or more following the birth of her child are highly unlikely to lose that weight. Women also have a higher propensity for tapping into emotional and social eating (see chapter 7, "How to Eat: Making the Most of Your Instincts").

Despite all these challenges, men still manage to gain weight. The term "beer belly" was coined expressly for men, but even if you don't like beer, all you need are excess calories. And once men cease exercising, their calorie-burning muscle will deflate quickly, lowering their metabolism into female ranges.

"I'm a banana!"

While women might be better at packing on the pounds, men can often *appear* fatter than women. Typically, men's bodies fall into the "apple" shape category while women are "pears." Apples tend to gain all their weight in the midsection, while pears pack it into the caboose. The good news for men is that the apple silhouette is more traditionally associated with fat, while a pear-shaped person is often simply referred to as "curvy."

Women can also gain toward the apple spectrum. To get an idea of what you'll look like at the end of your fat journey, examine the weight you already carry on your body. Are you heavier on the top and around the

Large Lingo: Cankle

An attractive leg line consisting of an uninter-
rupted span of corpulence from knee to foot,
eliminating the unattractive look of a tapered
calf and narrow ankle. Derived by combining the
words *calf* and *ankle*.

middle? You're an apple. Do you carry your
fat on your lower body? You're a pear. As
you gain, you'll delight in observing as your
natural shape becomes more exaggerated.

There's a little-known third category in the
fruit bowl, however: the "banana." Bananas
are tall and thin. If you fall into this group,
you'll probably have to eat larger quantities
and be even more inactive to elbow your
way into the apple or pear groups. But what
a thrilling surprise it will be when your
body makes its fat-distribution choice!

"I'm young!"

The differences between male and female weight-gain don't stop with metabolism or shape. Women put on an estimated 16 pounds between the ages of 25 and 54, while men gain roughly 10. For both genders, the most fat is added to the body between 25 and 34. Across the board, however, all of us experience a slowing of the metabolism as we get older, whether male or female. An aging body trades muscle for fat, which burns fewer calories. If you're dedicated and remain sedentary from now into retirement, you can expect your metabolism to wind down like an old clock.

That's no help for those who are young and active, however. If you're under 25, you may face a special set of challenges. They say that youth is wasted on the young; if you're

The Hunger Scale

Starving	
	1
Hungry	
	2
Could Eat	
	3
Satisfied	
	4
Full	
	5
Stuffed	
	6
Sick	
	7

Sometimes it's difficult to know how hungry or full you are. While you don't need to be hungry to eat, it's useful to assess your appetite to know whether you're eating as much as you possibly can. You should refer to the Hunger Scale throughout the day to rate your condition. If you're between 1 and 4, you should put down what you're doing and eat immediately, without stopping until you reach the 5 to 7 range. At the very least, you want to describe yourself as "full" after all your meals and snacks. If you ever allow yourself to go down to a 1, take the opportunity to gorge yourself on high-fat, sugar-rich foods. Not only is this physically pleasing and calorically productive, as an added bonus, you'll trick your metabolism into slowing down; your body will think it's starving and hoard fat.

young, you'd retort that fat is wasted on the old. At the risk of repetition, however, we can assure you that the laws of thermodynamics are behind you: eat more than you expend and you will gain, no matter your age.

"I just can't put on those last 50 pounds!

If you're already overweight, *How to Get Fat* will help you tip the scale into morbid obesity. Those of you who have never been thin, however, may face a unique problem. Have the terms "curvy," "husky," and "pleasantly plump" ever hurt your feelings? By now you should realize that's because they're euphemisms for *slightly* overweight. No wonder they sting—they imply that you haven't reached your goals. By the time you finish implementing this get-fat plan, you'll have a physique that even the most tactful person could never refer to as "big-boned."

No More Excuses

Excuses are natural, especially when faced with a daunting personal goal. The fact that you're reading this book, however, indicates that you long to make an important change in your life, and that means no more excuses. Hopefully these deconstructions of popular misconceptions have helped you into the mindset you'll need. Now it's time to get down to brass tacks—setting your goal weight and determining just how much food you'll need to eat.

CHAPTER 4

DETERMINING FOOD INTAKE: SETTING YOURSELF UP TO SUCCEED

TO ACHIEVE YOUR WEIGHT-GAIN goals, you'll need to understand the basic properties of caloric intake in order to develop a plan that will quickly and effectively add pounds to your body. For those of you who hated science and math, be forewarned that there are a few biological principles and formulas to learn, but we'll walk you through it step by step—as easy (if not as tasty) as pie. We'll show you:

- How to calculate your BMI and set your goal weight.

- How to determine your minimum caloric intake.

- How to adjust your eating for unplanned physical activity.

- Why golfing (with a cart) and sailing will help you achieve your weight goals more quickly than spin classes and cross-country skiing.

Setting Your Goal Weight

Before you can begin to productively enlarge, it's important to assess where you are and where you want to go. There are two methods to help you determine your weight-gain parameters. The first, a quick calculation, will yield the desired weight range for your height through a simple formula, giving you a ballpark target for the scale number you need to exceed. The second—and more reliable—barometer of fat is the body mass index (BMI). This

number addresses fat alone. Once you
tabulate your present weight, you'll have a
better idea of the journey ahead.

Quick Goal-Weight Calculation

Women

a. Start with 100 pounds for 5 feet.

b. Add 5 pounds per inch over 5 feet.

c. Subtract 5 pounds per inch under
   5 feet.

d. Add 50 to 75 percent.

Example: A woman with a height of
5 feet 2 inches:

100 lbs. + (5 lbs. × 2 in.) = 110 lbs.

110 lbs. + 50% = 110 + 55 = 165 lbs.

110 lbs. + 75% = 110 + 82.5 = 192.5 lbs.

Goal weight: 165 to 192.5 lbs.

Men

a. Start with 106 pounds for 5 feet.

b. Add 6 pounds per inch over 5 feet.

c. Subtract 6 pounds per inch under 5 feet.

d. Add 50 to 75 percent.

Example: A man with a height of 6 feet 2 inches:

106 lbs. + (6 lbs. × 14 in.) = 190 lbs.

190 lbs. + 50% = 190 + 95 = 285 lbs.

190 lbs. + 75% = 190 + 142.5 = 332.5 lbs.

Goal weight: 285 to 332.5 lbs.

If you're not yet overweight, the initial calculation probably represents something close to your current weight, while the percentages indicate where you need to go. Don't discourage if you're on the lower end—you may have a long road ahead, but you can do it!

Body Massive Index (BMI)

While stepping on the scale is an easy way to watch your weight balloon, the number between your toes includes fat, bone, muscle, and water. BMI gives a more accurate impression of an individual's fatness by comparing your weight to your height. Consult the BMI chart to determine where you fall in the spectrum:

	Body Massive Index (BMI)											
	Skin & Bones			Underweight			Pleasantly Plump			Gloriously Fat		
BMI	19	21	23	25	27	29	31	33	35	37	39	41
5'	97	107	118	128	138	148	158	168	179	189	199	209
5'2"	104	115	126	136	147	158	169	180	191	202	213	224
5'4"	110	122	134	145	157	169	180	192	204	215	227	238
5'6"	118	130	142	155	167	179	192	204	216	229	241	253
5'8"	125	138	151	164	177	190	203	216	230	243	256	269
5'10"	132	146	160	174	188	202	216	229	243	257	271	285
6'	140	154	169	184	199	213	228	242	258	272	287	302
6'2"	148	163	179	194	210	225	241	256	272	287	303	319

Height · Body Weight (lbs.)

If you prefer a more exact measure of your BMI, you can do the calculations yourself. The BMI formula was originally based on the metric system, hence the odd "703" figure; with this formula, we've spared you the rigors of conversion:

(Weight / Height^2) x 703 = BMI

Example: Starting weight of 140 pounds, height of 5 feet 6 inches:

(140 lbs. / 66 in.^{2}) × 703 = 0.032 × 703 = BMI of 22.6

Large Lingo: Saddlebags

Attractive bulges affixed to the upper region of a woman's outer thighs, supplementing an inadequate hip curve; can be used as handholds during sex, somewhat like the male *love handles*.

Once you know your BMI, you can set your goal number. The Centers for Disease Control defines normal weight as a BMI range of 18.5 to 24.9, while obesity is 30 or above. Whatever BMI you choose to strive for, you should not go under 25. Follow these guidelines when making your choice:

a. Skin & Bones: BMI under 25

b. Underweight: BMI of 25–29.9

c. Pleasantly Plump: BMI of 30–36.9

d. Gloriously Fat: BMI of 37 and above

You can also set your goal weight then work backwards to determine your goal BMI.

Example: Goal weight of 250 pounds, height of 5 feet 6 inches:

(250 lbs. / 66 in.^{2}) × 703 = 0.057 x 703 =

Goal BMI of 40.3

Calculating Minimum Necessary Calories

Again, we bring up the laws of thermodynamics: you must consume more than you expend in order to gain weight. Very few of us, however, know how many calories we burn in the course of normal daily life. To do that, you need to calculate your basal metabolic rate (BMR), the calories you need to keep your vital organs functioning:

Women: Current weight × 10 = BMR

Men: Current weight × 11 = BMR

Because few of us are fortunate enough to perform zero physical movement, however, you'll need to factor in your activity level and your digestion—because eating burns calories, too (see chapter 9, "Cease All Exercise: The Sedentary Life")!

First, using the table below, find the activity level that best describes your lifestyle:

Daily Activity	Activity Level	Activity Factor
Manual labor by trade, playing team sports, running	Heavy (discouraged)	0.5
Heavy housework or gardening; tennis, dancing	Moderate (not recommended)	0.4
Restaurant work, childcare, golf, sailing, walking	Light (acceptable)	0.3
Office work, reading, watching television, driving, sewing	Very light (preferred)	0.2

Now factor this number into the Activity Calories formula:

BMR × Activity Factor = Activity Calories

Finally, you'll need to include digestion in the equation. Digesting food and absorbing nutrients accounts for 10 percent of your daily energy needs.

(BMR + Activity Calories) × 0.1 = Digestion Calories

Now you have all the pieces to put together your daily calorie minimum:

BMR + Activity Calories + Digestion Calories = Daily Calories Needed

Example: Jane weighs 150 pounds. She doesn't exercise and she has a desk job, but activities with her three kids, husband, and dog, place her at the "Light" activity designation. What calorie level will she need to exceed in order to gain?

BMR: 150 lbs. × 10 = 1,500

Activity Calories: 1,500 × 0.3 = 450

Digestion Calories: (1,500 + 450) × 0.1 = 195

Daily Calories Needed: 1,500 + 450 + 195 = 2,145

Now What?

Your daily calorie minimum reflects only the energy you need *to survive*. In order to get fat, you must eat a surplus of calories. There are 3,500 calories in a pound. If you want to gain one pound per week, you must increase your caloric intake by 500 calories a day (3,500 divided by 7 days). If you want to gain two pounds a week, you need to eat 1,000 extra calories a day, and so forth.

Example: Bob is 5 feet 11 inches and weighs 200 pounds, and, fortunately for him, his activity level is "Very Light." His goal weight is 300 pounds.

God Bless America

Perhaps you don't want to leave the country and move to the South Pacific to be among your kind. If you'd like to stay domestic and bump tummies with like-minded souls, following are the fat-friendliest states in the union, as well as states you'd best avoid:

Most Desirable States				Least Desirable States		
Rate	State	% Overweight		Rate	State	% Overweight
1	Mississippi	67.3		1	Colorado	54.5
2	West Virginia	65.4		2	Washington, DC	55.0
3	Kentucky	64.9		3	Vermont	55.8
4	Arkansas	64.7		4	Massachu-setts	56.1
5	Louisiana	64.6		5	Arizona	56.2
6	South Carolina	64.6		6	Utah	56.2
7	Alabama	64.5		7	Montana	57.5
8	Alaska	64.2		8	Connecticut	58.2
9	North Dakota	64.2		9	Nevada	58.8
10	Texas	64.1		10	New Jersey	59.2

Statistics from CalorieLab, "United States of Obesity Fattest States Ranking 2006."

If he gains 5 pounds per month, he will reach his goal in 20 months.

BMR: 200 lbs. × 11 = 2,200

Activity Calories: 2,200 × 0.2 = 440

Digestion Calories: (2,200 + 440) × 0.1 = 264

Daily Calories Needed: 2,200 + 440 + 264 = 2,904

Because 3,500 calories = 1 pound, Bob needs to take in 17,500 (3,500 × 5) calories more a month. Per day, this averages 583 (17,500 / 30) calories.

To accomplish the weight gain he seeks, Bob's total daily caloric intake must be 3,487 (2,904 + 583) calories.

However, as Bob gains, he will need to recalculate this amount. By the time he is 290 pounds, for example, just 10 pounds short of his goal weight, his daily caloric needs will be:

BMR: 290 lbs. × 11 = 3,190

Activity Calories: 3,190 × 0.2 = 638

Digestion Calories: (3,190 + 638) × 0.1 = 383

Daily Calories Needed: 3,190 + 638 + 383 = 4,211

This kind of precise planning is really only necessary for those who have trouble putting weight on and keeping it there. It's important to note, however, that as you gain, you'll need to consume more and more calories just to maintain your desired weight.

Do the Math

Congratulations—you've now got a goal weight and the calorie counts to get there! Knowledge truly is power. There's so much to look forward to—your clothes will get tighter, your face will look bloated in pictures, and people will ask you what's going on in your life. But it's not enough to know how many calories—next, you'll learn the tricks to choosing the fat-friendliest foods.

CHAPTER 5
WHAT TO EAT: DEVELOPING THE RIGHT HABITS

WHAT'S BAD IS GOOD AND WHAT'S good is bad. This mantra will help you develop the right habits for a lifetime of weight gain. Society has long bombarded us with messages about foods that are "good" for us and others that are "bad." Though *all* food is good food when you're trying to get fat, "bad" food will get you to your goal weight much faster, and fortunately, the "bad" foods taste much better. But don't worry—you won't have to make these judgment calls on your own. We'll show you:

- How to invert the USDA food pyramid.

- Why you substitute juice and soda for water.

- Why you should befriend butter.

- How the microwave can be an important tool in your quest to gain.

Fat Food Pyramid: The Building Blocks of Fat

Familiarizing yourself with the basic food groups will help you favor the foods that make you fat while eschewing those that don't pull their weight. To get a general sense of what your daily food group breakdown ought to be, consult the following Fat Food Pyramid, an inversion of the USDA's deprivation-motivated recommendations:

Fat Is Your Top Priority

If you look at the bottom of the pyramid, you'll see that fats, oils, and sweets should dominate your meals.

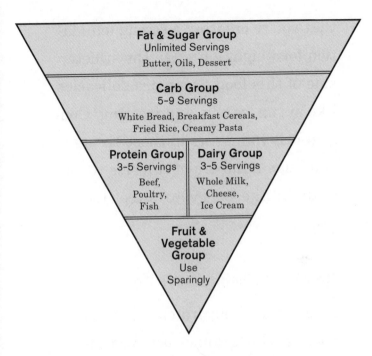

Fat & Sugar Group
Unlimited Servings

Butter, Oils, Dessert

Carb Group
5–9 Servings

White Bread, Breakfast Cereals,
Fried Rice, Creamy Pasta

Protein Group
3–5 Servings

Beef,
Poultry,
Fish

Dairy Group
3–5 Servings

Whole Milk,
Cheese,
Ice Cream

**Fruit &
Vegetable
Group**
Use
Sparingly

This is a no-brainer: fat gets you fat. Butter, margarine, and oil have about 100 calories *per tablespoon*! Because just a little bit of this food group will go a long way, think how far a lot will go. By keeping your focus on such fatty pleasures as bacon, pizza, and full-fat salad dressing, you can be confident that you're creating a strong foundation for weight gain. On the sweeter side of this food group are delicacies like syrup, candy, and frosting. Consistently indulging in these treats will add huge numbers of calories to your daily intake. Let your sweet tooth take the wheel!

Carbs: The Whiter, the Better

After fat, carbohydrates are your best friends. The "grains" section of the pyramid should be given high priority when you select your food. Although bread, cereal, rice, and pasta are featured, you'll want to focus on refined flour–based dishes like donuts, cookies, and muffins. Another reason to stick with refined flour is that whole grains can actually keep weight down. A study by the Harvard School of Public Health showed that 40 grams of whole grains per day decreased weight gain in middle-aged adults by as much as 3.5 pounds.

Animal Style

Once you've tackled your fats, carbs, and sugars, protein is next on the list, which includes animal products such as meat, poultry, fish, and eggs as well as other sources of protein like beans and nuts. Unless you make the mistake of choosing leaner cuts, red meat will offer you the highest fat content. While poultry and fish tend to be lower in fat than red meat, you can always augment these dishes with a condiment from the fat food group.

Say Cheese!

Dairy can be a very effective tool for weight gain, combining beautifully with carbs and meats to produce recipes like pizza that pack on the pounds. Increasingly, low-fat dairy products are dominating the food market industry. Rather than going for thin, tasteless facsimiles of milk, cheese, ice cream, and yogurt that have had the cream and fat—the best parts—removed, always choose full-fat renditions of your favorite dairy confections.

Spare the Produce

Fresh fruit and vegetables have little to offer in terms of calories and fat, so you'll want to be very judicious in your consumption of this food group. However, if you have a taste for fruits and vegetables, you can prepare them with heavy sauces, cheese, or sugar in order to get the most calories out of them. Alternatively, you can stick with such higher-calorie items as potatoes and dried fruits. Of course, there are important vitamins and minerals in produce, but it's nothing you can't replace with a multivitamin.

Drinking Your Calories: Eat, Drink, and Be Fatty!

By focusing too diligently on food, you could forget also to drink your calories. Beverages offer a quick and convenient way to ingest extra calories without filling up. Add soft drinks, sugary juices, alcohol, and caffeinated beverages to your daily routine to *drink* on more weight.

Convenience *and* Calories

Sodas and sugary juice drinks provide a large number of calories but feel like you haven't consumed much, leaving room for the calories you'll eat. A 12-ounce can of soda can provide you with 150 calories, while a supersize serving zooms above 400 calories and a Big Gulp can get you over 800! What's more, they're available practically everywhere—vending machines, convenience stores, gas stations, and movie theaters are stocked and ready to quench your thirst.

It used to be that diet and lite versions of your favorite drinks not only tasted different but *looked* different as well. Now, with improved artificial sweeteners, soft drinks and juices can taste quite similar to their high-sugar inspirations, and marketers exploit this with nearly identical packaging. Don't fall for the gimmick—keep a sharp eye out to avoid beverages packaged with slogans like "zero" and "only one."

Wake Up Your Caffeine Addiction

Since 90 percent of Americans consume caffeine on a daily basis, it stands to reason that it's helping us

Gendered Comfort

A 2003 University of Illinois study showed that the sexes differ in their definition of "comfort food." Men prefer dishes their mothers prepared for them, such as mashed potatoes, pasta, and meat, while women go for less labor-intensive, ready-to-eat treats, like candy, ice cream, and chips. The question remains: once the men are adults, who cooks their comfort food?

get fat. In addition to impairing our sleep (see chapter 2, "Changing Your Fat-itude: Getting into the Mindset"), thus making us fatter, caffeinated beverages are excellent vehicles for other fats and sugars. While black coffee won't get you anywhere, if you add whole milk and several spoonfuls of sugar, you're on your way. With a Starbucks on every corner, it's gloriously easy to take it a step further and add whipped cream and chocolate sauce.

Drink Your Dairy

It's a shame that most of us move away from drinking milk after childhood, because not only is it delicious and satisfying, it packs on the calories. Whether you consume the milk in your coffee drinks or cold out of the fridge, you'll be doing yourself a big favor. If you don't like plain milk, all the better—add chocolate! And don't forget the high watermark of caloric dairy consumption, milkshakes.

News Flash: Alcohol is Sugar!

In the same way that you can add fattening elements to caffeine, alcohol also blends beautifully with calorie-laden mixers. By itself, alcohol contains 7 calories per gram. With 12 grams in one shot of liquor, you've just downed an 84-calorie tequila shot! Add a sugary mixer and you can triple your caloric intake. Beer stretches the calorie benefits even further, with an average pint of lager weighing in at roughly 200 calories. And you may already be aware of a phenomenon from which snack-providing bartenders have been profiting for at least a century: munching salty snacks while drinking (e.g., peanuts, Goldfish, pretzels) not only allows you to take in food calories, it makes you want to drink more. In all, alcohol is a festive way to consume your daily minimum. Plus, it dehydrates you!

The Unbearable Irrelevance of Water

Depriving your body of water is a very common way for Americans to approach obesity. Water is a natural appetite suppressant because it helps the body metabolize fat. Ten glasses a day can undo all the work you've done to put fat on your body. Dehydration works in much the same way as starving and bingeing. Your cells panic, anticipating a lack of water. The water remaining in your system clings to those cells, causing swelling in your body. Water retention from alcohol, caffeine, and salt can help you look and feel fatter as you're gaining weight. Simply put, water contains no calories—why waste your time?

Cooking the Fat Way

You're about to learn how to shop for all the fattest foods, whether in a grocery store or at a restaurant. When prepackaged and prepared food loses its appeal, however, you'll want to go home and cook something fattening on your own. By doing it yourself, you'll find extra pleasure in knowing that you had a direct hand in sculpting your body. With the right tools in your kitchen and some high-fat tips, you can cook your way to obesity.

Kitchen Tools

While you want to add pounds, you're going to need to drop a few items from your kitchen. Ban measuring cups, measuring spoons, and kitchen scales from your cooking environment. You don't want any implements of portion control getting in the way of a fatter you. Next, clear your kitchen of non-stick skillets. These fat-sabotaging implements chemically eliminate the need for oil, butter, and other cooking fats. Use your old-fashioned skillets and keep the fat on high.

Nuke It

The microwave is the fat seeker's friend, especially those of us with busy lifestyles. Part of the challenge of successfully gaining is consuming enough calories over the course of the day, so time is of the essence. If you don't have enough time to cook and consume all the calories you need, you'll never meet your weight-gain goals. Microwaves speed up the process in every way, as well as allow you

---

Words of Plenty

"After a good dinner one can forgive anybody, even one's own relatives."

—Oscar Wilde

to rely on prepackaged foods. A few tips for the time-pressured: throw some tortilla chips, full-fat cheese, and refried beans in the microwave and you've got homemade nachos. Frozen pizzas and bowls of macaroni and cheese are a cinch. Reheat take-out, but be sure to add some oil, cheese, or butter to keep it moist the second time around. Zap your ice cream for 10 seconds when a craving hits and it'll be soft enough to scoop.

Recipe Substitutions

Whether recipes have been modified away from their high-calorie roots or they just don't incorporate enough fat and sugar, it's easy to bring them up to speed. If a recipe calls for anything low-fat, use the full-fat version instead. If baked goods include yogurt or applesauce, substitute lard. Almost anything is better with cheese on top or nuts inside, and there are few limits to what can be fried. When cooking, your basic rule of thumb should be to add fat, flour, and sugar whenever possible.

Pass the Grease

Now that you know your starting point and your goal weight, as well as what to eat and drink, you've made so much progress! It's time to go out there and procure your calories—in the aisles of the grocery store, at the tarmac of the drive-thru, brushing against the white linen of the restaurant. Once your eyes are opened to the world of fat, you'll be amazed how many purveyors out there want to help your cause.

CHAPTER 6
VITTLES GALORE:
BUYING THE RIGHT FOODS

FAT-INDUCING FOODS HAVE NEVER been so quick, inexpensive, and easy to procure. Supermarkets, convenience stores, and gas stations stock unlimited supplies of packaged snacks and fast foods to help you gain weight. Provided you have the right fattening ingredients, cooking at home can increase your calories and offer you a culinary adventure. And, of course, dining out is the most decadent way to add pounds. Wherever and however you find your food, adhering to some basic guidelines will keep you gaining. In this chapter, we'll show you:

- Why you want to grocery shop on an empty stomach.

- Why "white" foods are the "right" foods.

- How to spot and avoid no-no words like "skim," "low-fat," and "lite."

- What to order in a Japanese restaurant (hint—it's not sushi).

- How to become the Sherlock Holmes of the restaurant menu, searching for clues to the fattest selections.

Navigating the Grocery Store

The neighborhood bodega, the supermarket, the upscale food emporium—each holds wonderful opportunities to explore, taste, and buy. A few tips that will help you make the most out of every expedition:

- Go to the store hungry. With your stomach growling, you'll be more susceptible to food temptation.

- Don't make a list. Lack of preparedness leads to impulse buying and purchasing more food than you need.

- Use coupons. The savings will encourage you to purchase more food and you might be turned on to a new high-fat snack.

- Bring your kids. Their appetites will put sweets in your cart and their nagging will make you open snacks as you shop.

- Take advantage of free samples. Circle back for extra helpings. If the person in charge is stingy, let her know you're trying to get fat.

- Partake in last-minute shopping at the checkout counter. Those candy bars and sodas always look good!

> ## Enjoy Your Pancakes!
>
> A 1997 study at the University of Sheffield in the UK showed that fat-filled food reduces pain. Subjects who ate a meal of full-fat pancakes registered less discomfort in pain-sensitivity tests than those who ate low-fat pancakes. If the nutrients of the high-fat meal were ingested via a feeding tube, however, the pain was not reduced, underscoring the importance of sensory enjoyment.

How To Read Food Labels

The fat food pyramid in chapter 5 provided you with the basic information you need to prioritize your eating. But to determine whether specific foods you're consuming support your fat lifestyle, pay attention to the nutrition facts labels.

In 1990, the Food and Drug Administration (FDA) mandated that all packaged food products carry nutritional labeling. While it can be tedious to read the breakdowns of your favorite foods, knowing how to read a label will help you navigate the supermarket aisles. Once you've familiarized yourself with food ingredients, you won't need to read labels so closely, and you'll start to develop an instinct for which products are the most fattening.

In general, you'll want to go for "food products" rather than food. Giant agribusiness food-product manufacturers use a host of cheap, fattening ingredients such as hydrogenated oil and high-fructose corn syrup to improve texture, taste, and shelf life. Their quick blasts of blood sugar will drop quickly and soon have you hungry for the next fix—the so-called "false hunger cycle" (see chapter 7, "How to Eat: Making the Most of Your Instincts"). Who cares if it's false as long as it does the trick? Hydrogenated oil and high-fructose corn syrup are two of the things you'll be looking for when you read food labels.

Important Features of the Nutrition Facts Label

- **Total Fat:** This number will tell you whether you're getting enough fat. You want to keep your total fat well above 30 percent of your total calories. If your calorie minimum is 3,000, your daily fat requirement is at least 100 grams.

- **Calories:** Use this number to manage your daily calorie intake. Remember that the calories listed correlate to the stated serving size. The safest bet is always to eat everything in the package, as many products can be viewed as single servings in their entirety.

- **Dietary Fiber:** Choose foods with low fiber. Research shows that people who eat high fiber consume fewer total calories. A serving with 5 grams or more is considered to be high in fiber, so keep it under 4.

- **Ingredients:** Ingredients are listed in descending order; the first item, therefore, comprises the greatest percentage within the food. If you see butter, oil, high-fructose corn syrup, or refined white flour at the top of the list, that's a good indication of a snack for you.

In general you should steer clear of products that claim to have reduced fat, calories, and carbs. Food manufacturers stretch the truth at times, however, and the discerning shopper can learn to see through the false claims. Low-fat foods frequently pack a high number of calories: for instance, Lite Cool Whip has the exact

number of calories as the original variety
(25 per 2 tablespoons), making it an accept-
able substitute if the store is out of regular
Cool Whip. As a rule, however, try to avoid
any type of "reduced" food.

The Grocery Store: How to Shop

Shopping for food will become a religious
experience for you, because your local
supermarket is your new church. Aisle after
aisle of delectables offer you what you so
desperately need: fats, calories, and carbs,
all in bright packages at reasonable prices.

Making the grocery store your new mecca
might be a little overwhelming at first. A
general rule to bear in mind is that packaged, precooked, and frozen items are better
than fresh. If you must have fresh produce

and meats, purchase twice the amount you think you'll consume so that the anxiety over wasting fresh food will prompt you to eat more. Also remember to pick up all the condiments you'll need to boost their calorie yield. When it comes to color, try to stick in the white-beige-yellow arena, except if artificial dye is involved—these foods tend to be higher in calories as well as full of hydrogenated fats and high-fructose corn syrup.

With those tips in mind, let's learn some specifics on how to shop your way to fat.

Seeking Refinement

Whether or not you look at labels, it's relatively easy to spot foods made from refined, fattening ingredients. Grain products thicker in texture and darker in color house hidden fibers. If it's easy to chew, light in color, and slightly shiny in appearance, it's mostly likely a highly processed carbohydrate assembled with refined white flour.

Pick your pleasure: bread, cereal, pretzels, crackers, cookies—they each have entire dedicated supermarket aisles. Grab pasta, cake, and pastries. Wherever possible, make sure your choices pack an added punch of high-fructose corn syrup to trigger the false hunger cycle. If whole wheat or other whole grains are listed as the first ingredients, put the box back on the shelf.

Meat Market

When purchasing meat at the supermarket, keep an eye on the fat content. It's easy to slip up and select
meat that has been compromised.
With red meat, stick with marbled
cuts that allow you actually to see the
fat inside your purchase. In contrast,
beef labeled *lean* or *extra-lean* will rob
you of quality fat. Precooked whole
rotisserie chickens, an easy option for
families, come with their fat-dripping,
tasty skins intact. Although seafood
has less fat than other animal meats,
frozen fish and shrimp are often
breaded or combined with a creamy
sauce. Select tuna canned in oil
rather than spring water.

Subsidizing Your Fat

Fortunately for the weight-gainer, decades of American farm bills have reduced the cost of staple commodities such as corn, wheat, and soy with $25 billion a year in subsidies. These crops are the building blocks of packaged and processed foods—the very delectables that will help make you fat! Not to mention that the farm bills have wisely done little to support the renegade farmers who are wasting their time growing fresh produce. The result? No-no items such as lettuce and berries are 40 percent more expensive than they were in 1985, while the cost of sodas, rich in high-fructose corn syrup, fell 23 percent! Overall, delicious packaged goods made of corn-based sugar, wheat-based carbs, and soy-derived fat are increasingly affordable. It's never been easier to get fat on a budget!

Why Have Half When You Have Whole?

Like meat products, dairy items can be tricky. Avoid any containers with the words *skim*, *part skim*, *low fat*, *reduced fat*, or *fat-free* emblazoned on the packaging. Whole milk is what you want. Full-fat cheeses, especially the soft ones, rich in texture and flavor, will seduce your taste buds and pad your thighs.

Fruits and Veggies Made Over

Grocery stores offer myriad ways to turn fruits and vegetables into vessels of fat and calories. Fruits canned in sugar and syrup and vegetables and beans canned in oil and salt will raise the fat and calorie level of your favorite produce. Dried fruits and veggies are another excellent option because most of the water has been removed, condensing the nutrients and upping the calories per serving. Another way to eat your preferred produce is in jams, spreads, and dips. Raspberry jelly and spinach dip present a fattening transformation of previously low-calorie items.

For the diehard veggie lover, check out the supermarket salad bar and the deli case for sautéed or creamed veggies as an alternative to fresh. You can also try switching to starchy vegetables. Potatoes, squash, yams, and corn are more calorie-dense than asparagus, broccoli, and cucumbers, which are mostly water. And although most produce is virtually fat-free, avocado and coconut are two exceptions. When it comes to legumes, refried beans offer a high-fat option. And if you like nuts, buy a brand of peanut butter with added sugars and oils. Anything with *butter* in the name has to be fattening!

Shunning Foods that Fill

Certain foods make you feel fuller than others, depriving you of the opportunity to pleasurably eat more. Because dense, fiber-rich whole grains are harder to digest, they release energy into your body more slowly. Make a habit of staying away from weird grains like quinoa and amaranth that may be seem high in carbohydrates but ultimately force your total calories down. Fruits and veggies are also dangerous sources of fiber.

Eating Out Is Eating Fat: Restaurants and Fast Food

Dining out is an increasingly popular solution for the busy and the cooking-impaired. Not only has the price of prepared food dropped relative to ingredients over the last 30 years, there are so many more options: fast food, fast-casual (restaurants like T.G.I. Friday's and Applebee's), classic dine-in, delivery, and even supermarket-prepared foods. It's less fuss, and as an added bonus, it can be more calories.

The primary goal of restaurants is to make food that tastes good to customers, at a reasonable price. They know that fat, sugar, and salt are the way to a customer's taste buds, and customers will most likely have no idea the added calories are there. With fast food, price-cutting options mean hydrogenated fats and high-fructose corn syrup. And no matter what kind of restaurant, the emphasis on customer satisfaction and the knowledge of competition from other eateries means generous portions.

Fast Food: Fatter, Faster

Going to a fancy restaurant for a decadent meal will no doubt contribute to your obesity. But if you don't want to break the bank, take advantage of the prevalence of fast-food chains: convenient, ubiquitous, and cheap, not to mention equipped with drive-thrus, which help keep your energy expenditure down and allow you to eat in private. The average fast-food meal boasts 700 to 1,200 calories thanks not only to its high fat, sugar, and carb content but also to enormous portion sizes. Eat your fast-food meals until there's not a fry left, because enjoying fast food more than twice a week increases your likelihood of becoming obese by 50 percent!

Choose the Real Thing

Both fast-food establishments and high-end restaurants increasingly offer "healthy" alternatives to their regular fare. These dishes have often been stripped of calories and fat, and frequently have their own menu section or are marked with little symbols such as hearts, carrots, or the word "Lite." Be wary of these ploys. Become a menu sleuth and make sure your choice has the correct adjectives attached to it: "bathed," "coated," "fried," "crispy," and "creamy." If you're still confused about a restaurant's offerings, let the server know you're trying to get fat and ask him how something is prepared. He can tell you if your choice is too light for your needs.

Getting Fat with Any Cuisine

Just as bodies come in all shapes and sizes, food can appear in an astounding variety of cultural permutations. Be careful, though, because not all of it is fattening. Below are some general guidelines for getting fat on any cuisine:

	Choose	Avoid
Chinese	Fried foods, crispy noodles, sweet and sour dishes	Bean curd (unless fried), fish, hot and spicy dishes
Indian	Ghee, korma, molee, poori, samosas, naan	Dahl, masala, matta, paneer, raita, tandoori
Italian	Alfredo, carbonara, parmigiana, prosciutto	Marinara, clam sauce, wine sauce, picatta
Japanese	Tempura, agemono, katsu, sukiyaki, rice	Miso, sashimi, sushi, mushimono, yakimono
Mexican	Chimichangas, guacamole, sour cream, cheese, tortillas	Fajitas, ceviche, chili, gazpacho
Thai	Coconut-milk soup, peanut sauce, mee-krob	Fish sauce, sizzling meats, bean thread noodles, sate

Tips for Dining Out

- Choose fried, sautéed, and creamed over baked, broiled, and steamed.

- Add butter and salt to all dishes (even before you taste them).

- Order multiple appetizers.

- Don't waste your precious stomach space on dinner salads.

- Never agree to share an item; always order your own.

- Make the most of the bread basket (ask for one if it's not offered).

- Choose creamy soups and salad dressings.

- Add cheese when appropriate.

- Don't forget dessert.

Large Lingo: Love Handles

Squeezable folds of fat around the waist that amplify the sexiness of one's hips and lower back; can be used for gripping in the bedroom.

- If you order more than you can eat, bring the overflow home in a "doggy" bag. However, it's always better to push yourself to finish a meal rather than rely on leftovers.

The Well-Stocked Larder

Your cupboards should be full by now, and your local restaurateurs familiar with your rapidly plumping face. But how will you eat it all? Next, we'll show you how to harness your intuition to eat on occasions you never before associated with food, stretching your stomach to its maximum capacity.

CHAPTER 7

HOW TO EAT:
MAKING THE MOST OF YOUR INSTINCTS

WHEN EATING TO GAIN, THE MOST important thing to remember is not to rely solely on hunger. Hunger will prompt you to consume the calories you need to survive, and you want to do so much more than survive.

Instead, you'll be tapping other basic dynamics, like taste, emotion, and reflex. Taste will propel you to indulge past the hunger threshold, as when you're not hungry but hanker for a piece of chocolate. When tickling your taste buds isn't enough, you'll want to develop multiple reasons for eating: fear, sadness, celebration, boredom. These eating occasions fall into two categories: reflex-eating, wherein you eat because you're used to eating at those times; and self-soothing, when you use food to boost dopamine levels and feel emotionally full as well as physically. If you're unfamiliar with these consumption triggers, you'll be surprised how easy they are to incorporate into your daily life. Eating beyond hunger will prove invaluable to your fat quest. Here's what you'll learn:

- How comfort foods cause the acceleration of warm feelings.

- What specific foods to eat when you're angry, happy, or sad.

- How to set up your environment to ensure you indulge in unconscious eating.

- How to make food your go-to reward and substitute for human connections.

Comfort Food: Happy or Sad

When a baby cries, a mother gives her infant milk. When a toddler falls and bumps his head, a cookie is the antidote to his tears. Whether or not you're currently making the most of your emotional-eating potential, rest assured that the behavior has been imprinted on your psyche since birth.

Working with you is your own brain chemistry. Carbs and binge eating result in the release of dopamine. Part of the brain's rewards system, dopamine helps us learn to seek pleasurable outcomes—for example, it is also released during sex. Dopamine will soothe you and elevate your mood, an added bonus to the overeating that will get you fat.

Emotion can be a chief motivator for eating. Enjoying your favorite treats can commemorate a happy event or function as a salve for an insult or bad day. If you use food as an accelerator of good feelings and a cure for bad feelings, you'll be gloriously heavy in no time.

If You're Happy and You Know It, Take a Bite!

Food is a steadfast companion for happiness, whether celebration, nostalgia, or escape. With so many reasons to partake and imbibe, the more you party, the higher your calorie intake.

Birthdays and holidays, anniversaries and family reunions, birth announcements and engagements: all events to celebrate with a big meal. Weddings are the best opportunity to gorge on rich foods and drink. Be sure to keep an eye out for the cake, as many revelers are too drunk or distracted to notice when their slice lands in front of them. Snatch a few extra pieces before the band plays its encore.

Good food is strongly associated with good company (see chapter 8, "Where to Eat: Setting the Stage for Weight Gain"). When you're relaxed and with your friends, give in to the impulse to

Zap Your Blues with Carbs!

When eating lots of carbs makes you feel better, it's not just emotional. Carbs—especially when consumed without protein to drag them down, according to MIT researchers—increase the serotonin production in your brain, and they're just about the only things that can (naturally, that is)! Serotonin boosts your mood and soothes your irritability—some have called it the "feel-good" chemical. That means bread, cookies, and cakes not only taste good, they give you a natural high as well! To use this dynamic to your weight-gain advantage, rely on carbs to alleviate your melancholy when you're feeling sad, and keep them coming to regulate your mood overall.

graze and sip. Load up your plate at backyard barbecues and make sure you sample every hors d'oeuvre at cocktail parties.

Vacations—especially cruises—provide once-in-a-lifetime opportunities to gorge yourself. Of course, on the get-fat plan, this won't be too different from the way you're eating at home. When you're changing your eating lifestyle, varying circumstances shouldn't impact your successful overeating habits. However, vacations do afford exotic meals, luscious desserts, and, in the case of cruises and Las Vegas, 24-hour all-you-can-eat buffets, so they represent a perfect opportunity to gain.

You Deserve a Treat: Food Rewards

Learn to view food as a little gift to yourself. If your boss commends you on your performance at work, congratulate yourself with a steaming bowl of creamy pasta with buttery garlic bread. If you survive a harrowing trip to the dentist, grab a milkshake to soothe your beleaguered mouth. No reason is too small. By conditioning yourself to associate food with achievement, you'll set in motion a cycle of weight gain *and* succeeding in other spheres of your life.

Food Blues

What goes up must come down. At the other end of the emotional spectrum are anger, stress, and depression. While these feelings may be

Eating Your Feelings

For those of you who routinely process your emotions without using food to help, you may want to start an "Eating Your Feelings" journal to encourage mood-prompted feasting. This record will help you become aware of the emotional moments that yield the highest food intake for you. Take a look at this sample log to get you started. Whether you're happy or sad, try your best to eat as an expression of your feelings.

Trigger	Emotion	Old Reaction	New Reaction
Friday, 7:46 PM Broke up with boyfriend.	Sadness, self-loathing	Called a friend, talked for two hours, then took a bath and climbed in bed with magazine.	Pint of almond fudge ice cream with whipped cream
Monday, 5:32 PM Got a raise at work.	Happiness, pride	Enjoyed a pedicure and went out dancing.	Steak dinner with mashed potatoes and crème brûlée
Saturday, 9:13 AM Worried about terrorism.	Anxiety, fear	Went to gym to work off nervous energy, read about world policy on treadmill.	Large deep-dish meat lover's pizza

unpleasant, they create an urgent
need for emotional eating.

Unavoidable and unplanned upheavals
in life such as divorce, getting fired,
or the death of a loved one can be
transformed into weight gain as you
assuage your distress with food. But
big tragedies are few and far between,
so look to the day-to-day worries that
everyone faces. These eating triggers include love, aging, general work
stress, and finances. You're bound to
find something upsetting that will
make a candy bar a necessity.

If you're in a pinch and everything in
your life is going well, you can always
watch the news. The plight of the
world—gang violence, global warm-
ing, genocide—will wreak havoc on

your fat-sabotaging emotional stability, with the added bonus of keeping you in front of the television.

Hello, Drama Queen!

Now that you're familiar with the gamut of food feelings, you'll want to find the nuance in how emotional eating works for you. What makes you happy? What makes you sad? Awareness of your patterns will help you ingrain consistent fat-producing behavior.

Note that the food you reach for is often a literal representation of the feelings you're experiencing. Crunchy, salty chips when you're angry. Creamy, comforting ice cream when you're sad. Cake with sprinkles when you're happy. If you're not used to monitoring your feelings, look at what's in your mouth as an indicator.

Hand to Mouth: Unconscious Eating

One of the very best ways to consume extra calories is via unconscious eating, generally defined as snacking while you're doing something else, without regard for quantities, often out of the package, and without expressly enjoying or noting what is going into your mouth. While this type of eating comes naturally to many, you can also train yourself to lose track of the quantities you consume.

A few examples of unconscious eating include snacking when you're bored, grazing throughout the day, and munching while watching television. To promote unconscious eating, start with a large

quantity of food, generally a complete package that contains many recommended servings. Choose another activity to focus on
while you eat, then allow your mind to drift
or engage with your other activities. As
long as you keep snacks handy, you can eat
unconsciously anywhere, anytime.

Activities that Promote Unconscious Eating

- Watching television.

- Going to a movie.

- Working on the computer.

- Hanging out with friends.

- Surfing the Internet.

- Talking on the phone.

- Driving.

Triggering Shame Spirals

A shame spiral is a world-class gateway to eating. Most people have experienced shame spirals, but few know how to trigger them deliberately and channel their considerable energy into binges.

Shame spirals are internal emotional meltdowns in which each bad thought leads to five more until it's impossible to pull out of the vortex of self-hatred. This may sound unpleasant, but the resulting eating is so satisfying, not to mention calorie-rich, that it's worthwhile for the gainer (especially if you've hit a plateau).

The key to triggering shame spirals is inviting drama into your life as well as cultivating your knowledge of aspects of yourself that you don't like. When it's time for a good shame-based binge, get your food ready—be sure that you've got enough, then buy some more. Next, identify a shame source and initiate contact. Examples include calling your mother, intentionally running into an ex-lover, and attending your high school reunion. When the first feelings of distress emerge, recite the traits you detest in yourself then blame yourself for all that's gone wrong. When you feel like you just can't drop any lower, begin eating and don't stop until the food's gone.

- Reading.

- Procrastinating.

- Cooking (a primo grazing opportunity).

- Watching someone else cook.

Every Meal Is Thanksgiving

Even if you're a slave to the fat food pyramid and nutrition facts labels, if you eat only until you're satisfied you'll run the risk of maintaining a stable, moderate weight. If you eat when you're hungry and stop when you're not, however, don't be ashamed: your brain chemistry is at fault, not your willpower. You can train yourself to eat past the feeling of fullness, trigger false hunger, and maximize cravings, and achieving your desired weight gain will be within reach.

The "Hippo" in Hypothalamus

The hypothalamus is the area of the brain that processes eating behavior. When your stomach is physically full of food, a chemical called cholecystokinin sends signals to the hypothalamus. By consistently eating huge quantities of food, especially quickly, however, you can desensitize your cholecystokinin mechanism. Your brain will eventually overlook feelings of fullness. You may feel nauseous or experience heartburn when you begin imprinting this habit—this is normal. Sip some ginger ale, take a Tums, or lie down. After a few binges you'll develop the stamina you need.

Hunger Is a State of Mind

In addition to cholecystokinin, two hormones have been linked with hunger and appetite. When your stomach is empty, ghrelin is secreted to alert your brain of your body's pressing need for food. Once you're full, leptin is released so that you stop

How to Get Stuffed

Given that you want to stay in the top range of the Hunger Scale (see page 61), at full, stuffed, or sick, use these tips to make sure your stomach is always at maximum capacity:

- Eat quickly.
- Eat when it's time to eat, whether or not you're hungry.
- Eat when you're alone.
- Eat when other people are eating.
- Always have seconds (and thirds).
- Always have dessert.
- Always clean your plate.
- Always clean others' plates.

eating. High-fructose corn syrup, however, inhibits leptin secretion so that
your brain never gets the message
that you're full. This miracle sweet-
ener also keeps the ghrelin flowing so
that you continue to feel hungry even
though you have food in your stomach, two more excellent reasons to
consume as much high-fructose corn
syrup as possible (see chapter 6, "Vittles Galore: Buying the Right Foods").

Maximizing Cravings

While hunger is a biological reaction,
there are eating needs that go deeper.
A craving occurs when you desire
a specific type of food at a certain
time. Researchers have found that
hormones, gender, emotional connection to the food, and time of day

are involved. Afternoon and evening are prime craving times. For women, pregnancy and premenstrual syndrome offer terrific opportunities for craving exploitation. When a craving hits you, make the most of it. Listen to your inner voice. What would hit the spot? Yield to that whim as quickly as possible. (Be sure to stock large quantities of frequently craved foods in case the spirit moves you.)

The Next Best Thing: Replacement Eating

Eating can replace just about everything. It can fill any void in your life, especially the absence of human connection. Food provides unconditional love. A piece of cheesecake won't turn you down for a promotion. A double cheeseburger can't leave you for a younger woman. And a box of glazed donuts will never lie. You can trust food.

The more you learn to rely on food as your sole support, the more weight you will gain. As you advance along this path, you may find yourself out with friends wishing that you were at home eating an entire bag of chips followed by a pint of ice cream. If this happens to you, congratulations! You've just advanced to a new level in your quest to gain.

Food can also replace other destructive activities, such as shopping. The next time you feel like going on a credit-card-maxing spree, try eating instead. If you wish you could go to a concert with friends but have to work late, buy something from the office vending machine. It's a bait-and-switch method that almost always works.

Find Full-fillment

When you started on this program, you probably thought we would address food as fuel for fat, but now you're seeing that it's so much more. Food can comfort, distract, reward, and fulfill. You've not only gained yourself an eating plan, you've made a new friend, lover, and pastime. When you allow food to be your life partner, you'll enjoy a lifetime of fat. But where will you and this partner live, work, and play? Read on to learn how to stage your environments for maximum eating.

IF YOU COULD LOCK YOURSELF UP IN a closet with a lifetime supply of pizza and ice cream, getting fat would be simple. Unfortunately, you can't work toward your goal weight and BMI in a vacuum. Your home, work, and social environments must all play vital roles in helping you become obese.

Often a fat-seeker's own resolve to gain weight isn't what stands in his or her way. Fat-sabotaging conditions like a barren home pantry or an empty office refrigerator can undermine any overeater's progress, not to mention that negative influences like a self-denying family member or a carb-cutting coworker can be toxic to morale.

To combat these obstacles, you'll need to set yourself up to succeed. From your kitchen to your circle of friends, fat is the new focus. Taking steps to foster and maintain food-friendly surroundings will make a big difference in your push toward obesity. In this chapter, we'll share with you such tools and tips as:

- Putting tables and television sets in every room in your house.

- Stretchy pants: your best friend and a boon to overeating.

- Keeping a bowl of candy on your desk.

- Incorporating eating into even the most non-food-oriented activities.

Home Is Where the Food Is: Making Your Home Conducive to Eating

Your home environment will be the epicenter of your new fat lifestyle. As such, every aspect of your home must be geared toward eating. Stocking up on food, identifying delivery sources, creating a comfortable environment in which food is near at hand, and prepping your wardrobe will ease your transition to fat.

If It's There, You'll Eat It

Many meals are eaten at home, whether or not they're prepared there. In your personal living space you can enjoy comfort, privacy, and unlimited second helpings. Adequately overstocking your kitchen will create around-the-clock eating opportunities.

Buy in bulk so that you're never empty-handed. Stock up on your favorite indulgences so that no craving will ever go unsatisfied. Packaged foods and frozen items not only last longer on the shelf, they provide preparation speed and convenience. As an added bonus,

---

Chocolate Sex

Thanks to its chemical makeup, chocolate can be a satisfying replacement for sex. Chocolate contains phenylethylamine, which your brain releases when you experience such physiological manifestations of love as a pounding heart and tummy flutters. Some researchers say that chocolate also triggers the release of mesolimbic dopamine, a chemical present in the pleasure centers of the brain at the height of orgasm. Anandamide, another Hershey-friendly substance, can create a pleasurable feeling similar to the effects of marijuana or sexual afterglow. Chocolate's sweetness can increase elation-causing endorphins. Why bother with sex when there's chocolate?

when you open your freezer to grab
a microwaveable fettuccine Alfredo,
chances are that the rocky road will
also catch your eye. Treat your refrigerator as though it has a revolving door.

If for some reason you're left in the
lurch with no food in the house, takeout
is always an option. Keep a variety of
menus on hand to suit any mood. Favor
restaurants that require a minimum
purchase amount so that you must add
a dessert, an appetizer, or a second
entrée. In fact, why not order several entrees to have on hand for later
tonight or tomorrow? Remember also
that many grocery stores now deliver.

Fat Shui

Once you have enough sheer calories
in your house, think about layout. Just

because the kitchen is ground-zero for food doesn't mean eating should be banned in other areas of your home, nor does it mean you can't also store food elsewhere for easy access.

Cultivate cozy eating areas all over the house. Make sure you have ample, plush seating. Place end tables and coffee tables nearby so that food can be enjoyed from every seat. Don't rule out putting mini-refrigerators in rooms far from the kitchen so you don't have to get up for a refill. Adding television sets to as many rooms as possible promotes a delightfully sedentary way of life.

Incorporate food into the décor of your residence. Plant distinctive cookie jars throughout your home. Bowls of chips, chocolates, or salted nuts can replace potpourri. And when setting out these methods of snack delivery, keep proximity to chairs, couches, and beds in mind.

Grow into Your Wardrobe

Take your wardrobe into consideration as you begin to gain. Just as you adapt your pantry and your furniture to suit your new lifestyle, tailor your closet as well.

By purchasing pants with elastic waistbands and clothing made with spandex and Lycra, you can avoid buying new outfits whenever you go up a size. Extra-large clothing that you can grow into (and anything with the word "tent" in it) is a wardrobe winner. Toss pieces made of leather, tweed, denim, or anything else that won't stretch. Cotton affords some wiggle room but you run the risk of shrinkage in the wash. Overall, avoid chafing and pinching to make your weight gain as pleasurable and easy as possible.

The only downside to oversized and stretchy items is that it's easy to lose track of how much you're gaining and miss out on the satisfaction that comes from feeling your clothes get tighter. To acknowledge your progress, keep one pair of skinny jeans and pull it out whenever you want a reminder of how far you've come.

Office and School: A Work-Study Program for Food

Unless you work from home, the food-friendliness of your office or school environment

Sleep-Eating

If you're like most of us, you've probably gotten up from bed in the middle of the night, unable to resist the lure of the cake in the fridge. However, few awaken in the morning shocked to see evidence of a binge they don't remember. These individuals are lucky enough to have Nocturnal Eating Syndrome, a sleep disorder in which a person sleepwalks to the kitchen, consumes vast quantities of food, and then goes back to bed without ever awakening. Presumably a response to stress, the episodes occur during non-REM sleep and, despite being followed by "daytime anorexia" due to the nighttime calories consumed, generally lead to obesity.

is just as important as the food conditions in your living space—after all, you probably spend more waking hours there than you do *chez vous*! From organizing office potlucks to keeping candy bars in your backpack, employ the same fat-seeking vigor in the outside world as you do at home.

Bring Home the Bacon

While you should stockpile food at home, you most likely won't have that kind of space at work. Get to know the food availability around you. Gather takeout menus from nearby restaurants—it's best to do this online in order to avoid unnecessary walking. A cafeteria or coffee stand is a terrific resource for snacking. At the very least, your building should have vending machine full of candy bars, sodas, and chips for your snacking pleasure. One good trick to keep yourself eating throughout the day is to place a bowl of candy on your desk in plain view of your coworkers. People will be sure to stop by for a treat and this will remind you to partake yourself.

We All Scream for Ice Cream

Social eating at work and school creates a more festive atmosphere and makes the process of gaining weight that much more pleasurable. Get to know the other gainers in your office and see what they have to share. If others bring in food, you don't always have to foot the bill in your quest for fat.

Take advantage of every opportunity for celebration, however insignificant, as a way to bring food into your office or school space. Birthdays are perfect excuses for cakes, cupcakes, and other sweets. If no one else has done so, take it upon yourself to compile your coworkers' birthdates and alert the others in advance so they feel compelled to bring treats. While this might seem like additional work for you, it will pay off when you gain those extra frosting pounds.

All the major holidays are occasions for office parties. People bring in bags of candy for Halloween and boxes of chocolate for Valentine's Day. Help step up the food sharing by organizing potlucks around everything from Cinco de Mayo to Black History Month. Traditional recipes are often more fattening because impoverished cultures needed to preserve the pounds. Appeal to your coworkers' religious and regional backgrounds and urge them to share dishes that represent their cultures.

Just as you can be a ringleader for food consumption in the office, you can be the same instigator in your

Large Lingo: Buddha Belly

Expansive, round stomach reminiscent of the popular icon's physique, which can be rubbed for good luck.

classroom or dorm. Rope your friends into eating and drinking as alternatives to studying. Suggest pizza breaks and midnight donut runs frequently and soon you'll become the go-to snack-runner for your procrastinating peers. And why not think up ways to incorporate eating with education? Suggest a "Delicacies of India" class to your geography instructor, a "Meals in Impressionist Paintings" session to your art history teacher, a "Chemical Experiments with Food Additives" study block to your science TA, a "Determining the Thermodynamic

Formulas for High-Calorie Foods"
puzzle to your Mathletes coach.

Table for One

Despite your best efforts to involve
coworkers or fellow students in your
gluttony, you might face the misfortune of working or studying with
people who share different values or
who are in denial about their own
need to gain weight (see chapter 2,
"Changing Your Fat-itude: Getting
into the Mindset"). Carbophobes
and fat naysayers can be prickly
about easy-access food, quashing all
attempts at community eating.

However small or large your personal
space at work or at school, ignore the
deprivation junkies and make over
your own area to suit your needs. If

you have an office, get yourself a mini-fridge and bring in your favorite snacks. If a desk is all you have, designate a drawer or three for foodstuffs. If you're a student or you work on the go, pack tasty, calorie-dense foods in your backpack. In a dorm room, however, be sure to label your food so that yo-yo-dieting roommates won't binge on your carefully gathered fat resources.

Social Eating vs. Dining Alone

Although you don't always have a choice when it comes to coworkers, your private life is your own. As discussed in chapter 2, social pressures can wreak havoc on your commitment to fatness. While it's important to surround yourself with people who support your choice to be fat, it's *vital* to eat only with those who understand your goals.

Let's Do Lunch

Once your friends and family know about your dedication to fat, you can involve them in the process. Let them know that all social interaction with you will be based around food. When you make plans, be sure the principal activity will consist of eating. Try fine restaurants, fast-food stops, pizza-and-movie nights, ice cream socials, wine tastings, picnics in the park, and so forth.

If you're cornered into a non-food-based activity, there are always ways to incorporate eating after the fact. If a friend asks you to a movie, suggest you lunch before or after. If she doesn't have time for a meal, make the most of the concession stand. If you're on a budget, stash store-bought

Redundantly Fatty

When everyday fatty foods aren't enough, seek out innovations that take your favorite snacks to the next level. County fairs, sweet shops, street vendors, and ballparks offer treats that feed two fat cells with one snack. These efficient delights generally consist of a food item that's already high in fat and calories which is then dunked, smothered, or encased in another fattening substance, resulting in at least twice the calories!

- **Deep-fried Twinkie:** Hostess cake dipped in batter, fried, and served on a stick.

- **Walking taco:** Taco meat, cheese, and sour cream dumped into an open bag of corn chips. Eaten with a fork.

- **Chocolate-dipped Oreo:** Twice the chocolate.

- **Chicken-fried steak:** Beef dipped in an egg-and-flour mixture then fried.

- **Turducken:** De-boned turkey stuffed with a de-boned duck, which is already stuffed with a de-boned chicken, which in turn has already been stuffed with a mixture of Cajun sausage and breadcrumbs.

- **Bacon burrito dog:** Flour tortilla wrapped around two hot dogs, two slices of cheese, three slices of bacon, and chili and onions.

treats in your pockets. Good planning and preparation will keep your calories up wherever you are.

Flying Solo

At times, eating alone will be the only way to ingest enough calories to reach your goal. Whether there's no one to dine with, your friends don't understand your lifestyle, or you live among a family of self-deprivers, never hesitate to carve out your own time and place to consume what you need. Whether it's storing candy under your bed so you can eat it after everybody's gone to sleep or stopping at the drive-thru then pulling over to wolf down your meal, *you* are the only one responsible for seeing that you get enough calories.

The Fat Lifestyle

Setting the stage for obesity involves more than just your own commitment. Your surroundings—both physical and emotional—must be in line with your new goals. Pat yourself on the back and breathe a huge sigh of relief now, because you're done with the work portion of the get-fat program. It's time to do nothing—or, more specifically, to not exercise.

CHAPTER 9
CEASE ALL EXERCISE: THE SEDENTARY LIFE

IF YOU FOLLOW THE ADVICE YOU'VE read so far, you'll undoubtedly add pounds to your body. But to go the extra mile and achieve maximum obesity, it's important to avoid miles all together—miles on foot, that is! A sedentary lifestyle will greatly increase the speed and efficiency of your weight gain.

Here's the plain truth about exercise: it *burns* calories—precious calories that you want to hoard so they'll blossom into fat cells. Exercise will slow, and possibly impede, your journey to fat. A study by the Centers for Disease Control revealed that a full 37 percent of obese people engage in zero physical activity. Clearly they understand the futility of exercise and have made a commitment to fat that goes beyond merely eating mass quantities of food. Learn from their example: sit still, get fat. In this chapter, we'll show you:

- Why fitness junkies lose their dignity.

- Ten excuses you can use with family and friends to get out of physical activity.

- How moving sidewalks, escalators, elevators, and golf carts will become your best friends.

- The single most fattening activity you can participate in.

Excising Exercise

For many fat aspirants, it won't be a problem to eliminate exercise from their lifestyles. The amateur athlete who sees a rigid no-exercise policy as the best kind of vacation will be off to a great start. The lucky folks who've never worked out a day in their lives are already there. For some, however, this aspect of the program can pose a problem. If you enjoy athletics despite the need to stop exercising, you can redirect this energy into more productive outlets by examining the reality behind your passion. And don't get discouraged: you're not the first reformed endorphin-junkie to turn muscle into jiggle.

Survival of the Fattest

There was a time when human beings needed to be fit to survive. Hunting for food, fleeing predators, propagating the species, and withstanding the elements required muscle, coordination, and stamina. But the caveman days are over, and the vast majority

Superstar Fat Cells

Scientists used to believe that fat cells were like the last kid picked in gym class: lazy, worthless, and unremarkable. But new research has fat cells scoring with the homecoming queen. Fat, it turns out, is highly active tissue with significantly more power than previously assumed. Now labeled an "endocrine organ" like the thyroid or pituitary glands, fat cells are the hub of an intricate communications network that controls the body's energy supply, possibly secreting more hormones and proteins than any other organ. Fat even tells the body when it can reproduce: emaciated fashion models, for example, cease menstruating because their fat cells have determined that more maternal padding is needed to sustain a healthy pregnancy. But the most astounding attribute of fat cells is their propensity to expand and multiply. Consistent overeating causes fat cells to swell. When they reach a breaking point, however, they don't divide, as a simpler cell might. Instead, they delegate by commanding immature cells to divide and produce more fat cells. Consequently, a thin adult might have approximately 40 billion fat cells while an obese individual can boast double or three times that amount—not to mention that the fat cells of an obese person are larger in size!

of us no longer have to farm our own food, walk anywhere, or move heavy machinery. With the bounty of food at our disposal, the only hunting we need to do is seeking out our favorite flavor of ice cream at the grocery store. The advent of modern transportation means you only have to walk a few feet to get anywhere in the world. There's no longer a functional reason for physical fitness. Toning your muscles and increasing your endurance is therefore a complete waste of valuable time that could be spent eating.

Debunking Fitness Culture

Let's face it—gyms are silly. With the obsolescence of physical fitness, athletic clubs only offer the opportunity to sweat, experience discomfort, and look like an idiot. Exercise junkies heaving on treadmills are no more than hamsters in wheels. Meatheads lift weights for no other purpose than to put them back down. Aerobics bunnies lose ten IQ points per bounce. Save your money and your dignity and ditch the gym.

This attitude extends to all forms of exercise. Outdoor running is ridiculous unless, of course, you're being chased, and if you're fat enough, you'll be able to overpower your pursuer with mere size anyway. Skiing makes you cold, surfing makes you wet, mountain biking hurts your bum. Sure, a good game of soccer or basketball could be fun. But is it more fun than grabbing a burrito? When you view exercise through the lens of fat, it's all pointless and demeaning.

Give Your Metabolism a Break

If you don't cease the sweat, you'll speed up your metabolism and rob yourself of caloric impact. A sedentary person can gain weight when consuming 1,800 calories per day or less! Athletes, on the other hand, might burn 5,000 calories in a day. With repetitive exercise, you run the risk not only of burning calories while active but also generating lean muscle, which continues to allow calories to escape long after you've stopped moving. Don't risk your hard-won progress: kick the exercise habit, slow down your metabolism, and gain some more weight.

The Ol' Bait and Switch

If, against all reason, you love to exercise, here are a few tips to disabuse yourself of

> ## Words of Plenty
>
> "It's simple. If it jiggles, it's fat."
> —Arnold Schwarzenegger

this damaging habit. Diversion tactics will help get you over the exercise hump, operating the same way as replacement eating (see chapter 7, "How to Eat: Making the Most of Your Instincts"). When you want to work out, eat instead. If you don't feel like eating, don't chastise yourself; instead, try a sedentary activity like taking a nap, reading, going to a movie, talking with friends, or surfing the Internet. Another outlet for your desire to exercise is spectator sports. Adopt a team and begin rooting for them. Be careful not to get too excited, though; you'll want to keep the cheering verbal and not physical when your team scores a goal.

When You Need an Excuse

All the planning the in world won't save you from the perils of peer pressure. At some point, you'll inevitably find yourself boxed into an exercise corner. You rent a beach house with friends and everyone wants to play volleyball. You join a family picnic and the kids want you to lead a hike. If those around you don't understand or know about your quest for fat, be prepared with alternate reasons for refusing to participate.

10 Excuses to Get Out of Physical Activity

1. Don't have the right clothes or equipment.

2. Too hot, too chilly, might rain.

3. Need sunscreen.

4. Have a cold; getting over a cold.

5. Low blood sugar (need to eat).

6. Injury (preexisting or suddenly occurring).

7. Heart condition.

8. Menstrual cramps (works well with men).

9. Allergic to grass.

10. Ate within the last 30 minutes (fear of cramping).

Culture of Convenience

For a fat-seeker committed to a sedentary lifestyle, getting fat can happen quickly and naturally. But not everyone can sit around all day. Some of us have jobs or personal commitments that require movement (see chapter 2, "Changing Your Fat-itude: Getting into the Mindset"). Thankfully, there are many strategies to help you navigate these hurdles and decrease your physical activity. One of the beauties of Western civilization is the way it's removed the necessity for strenuous activity from our day-to-day lives; you need only take advantage of it.

Why Walk When You Could Drive?

No trip is too short to justify driving. Choosing the car over walking—*every* time—is one key factor in successful weight gain. Be sure to park close to your destination, even if it means circling the parking lot a few times (better to waste gas than calories). Valet park whenever possible.

Machines Do the Work For You

Say yes to golf carts. At airports, step on the moving sidewalks and ask to be transported to your gate in one of those beeping carts. In department stores, ride the escalator, and in office buildings, take an elevator—*never* use the stairs. If you don't see an escalator or elevator, ask an employee where it is, as most buildings are required to have accommodations for the disabled. Your weight gain is your most important goal, so if you must, develop a limp and lie about your able-bodied capabilities to avoid exertion.

Let Others Burn Calories

Whenever possible, let someone else do it. Allow bellboys to carry your luggage and accept the supermarket clerks' offers to help you get your groceries to your car. It's their job—who are you to keep them from performing it? For women, chivalry can go a long way toward getting you fat—if a gentleman offers you his seat on the subway, take it!

Expand upon this mentality at home. Think ahead when snacking in front of the television and limit trips between the fridge and the couch. If someone else gets up, use the old "While you're up" tactic and make them fetch what you need. Invest in appliances of convenience such as dishwashers and employ a cleaning service to avoid

performing strenuous housework yourself. Do anything and everything to
keep yourself seated and relaxed.

The Fattest Inactivity of All

Research shows that watching television is
the most fattening of all inactive activities
(fortunately for weight-seekers, it's entertaining, too!). A 2002 study in the *Journal
of the American Medical Association* pro-
filed 50,000 female couch potatoes. Scientists found that for every 2 hours an adult
woman spent in front of the television,
obesity increased by 23 percent. Zoning out
in front of the television will put on the
pounds faster than driving a car, sewing, or
sitting at a desk. And Americans are leading the way, averaging about 30 hours of
television watching per week.

Inertia: A Human at Rest Tends to Stay at Rest

The motivations to remove all exercise from your lifestyle are many: physical activity burns calories, speeds up your metabolism, and robs you of fat. Not exercising is particularly helpful if you're consuming all your required calories but still not gaining as fast as you'd like; sitting still will be just the extra boost you need to get you past your plateau. Do nothing and the pounds will come to you!

Fat isn't just for today, however—it's a lifelong choice. When you're initially gaining, momentum and excitement will support your progress, but after you've been living with fat for a while, it can become challenging to keep the pounds on long-term. Next we're going to examine the skills you'll need to cement your dream—for life.

CHAPTER 10
CONCLUSION:
TAKING FAT TO THE NEXT LEVEL

CONGRATULATIONS, YOU BEAUTIFUL fatty—you've completed the program! While being fat is certainly reward enough, you must pat yourself on the back for your resolve and determination in turning your fantasy into reality. While we'd like to say that this is the end, it's really just the beginning. It's easier to stay fat than it is to get fat, but keeping your weight up requires vigilance nonetheless. Before we explore your maintenance plan, however, it's important to take a moment to assess the impact of your success.

Your personal fulfillment should always take priority over the exact size of your body. Perhaps you've hit your exact goal weight, or maybe you've still got a few pounds to go. Or it's possible that you reached a weight that was perfect for you even though it was under what you'd initially designated as "perfect." The true accomplishment of your journey is recognizing the control you've taken over your body and your life and knowing that you can achieve anything you set your mind and mouth to. And above all, loving yourself, no matter your size. Keeping this kind of perspective will allow you to make peace with the level of fatness that's right for you.

Reaching your goal is thrilling and you should revel in the feeling of accomplishment. But staying there is just as important, if not more so, than getting there. Don't squander your success. Look at your goals with realism and flexibility. Address setbacks quickly, rationally, and effectively. Surround yourself with positive support. Follow this maintenance plan and you'll be making fat your choice for life.

Maintenance: Fat for Life

While reveling in all that you've achieved, you'll need to be careful not to backslide into thinness. Now that you've put the weight on, let's keep it on. A weight maintenance plan should be put into effect after you've reached your goal weight. You don't want to make the common mistake of forgetting all you've learned and reverting to an active, under-nourished lifestyle. For maintenance, you'll want to remember the three B's: be aware, be consistent, and be still.

Be Aware

Seeing your goal weight on the scale and finally calculating that top-level BMI doesn't end your fat story: it's important to keep an eye on those stats and make sure they stay put. Studies show that successful weight-maintainers are able to catch that 5 to 10 pound backslide before it transforms into all-out weight loss.

Weigh yourself regularly, at the same time of day and in the same clothes. Calculate your BMI at least once a month, if not more. Catch any loss of more than 2 pounds and reverse it with some deliberate excess. As an added bonus, this type of vigilance will cause hunger-inducing anxiety.

Be Consistent

If you've come this far, you've done something right. Observe and acknowledge the routine that has worked for you. Make a list of your go-to foods and keep it on your fridge. Sit and think about ways you've effectively avoided physical exertion. Outline your most productive triggers for eating. Seeing factors like these on paper will ingrain them further

Eat Your Way to Peace!

If you're overweight by United States military standards, not only are you prohibited from enlisting, you won't be drafted should conscription be reinstated. Each service branch has its own guidelines, disqualifying some 40 percent of women and 20 percent of men of recruiting age. And once you're in, they keep watching you: in 2003, the military discharged over 3,000 people for weight gain.

into your psyche. You've done a great job—just make sure it stays the *same* job and you'll stay the same size.

Be Still

Even if you're already avoiding fitness, look for additional ways to refrain from exertion and hoard calories. Assess your environment with fresh eyes. New shortcuts? A hidden elevator? Try clipping a pedometer to your belt and keep track of how few steps you can take in a given day, and challenge yourself to reduce it by 10 steps per day.

Setbacks, Plateaus, and Falling Off the Wagon

Even the most aware, consistent, and inactive morbidly obese person will have a bad day. Setbacks and plateaus are pitfalls you're bound to face. Because they're inevitable, your reaction makes all the difference— recover and nip it in the bud! Studies show that people who can keep their weight stable are problem-solvers. Fending off defeatist attitudes and returning to the fight with renewed vigor will keep obesity in your life.

Slow and Steady Wins the Race

It's a classic bad day. Running late causes you to skip your morning French toast with syrup and forget your mid-morning chocolate muffin at home. To your horror, the catered lunch at work is fish and steamed vegetables. Then your car breaks down and you have to *walk* to a gas station. By the time you get home, all the pizza-delivery chains are closed and you haven't made it to the grocery store in a week. Feel like you want to give up and drop the weight? Wrong!

Expect that you'll have moments when relinquishing your fat habits is beyond your control. And sometimes, maintaining the fat lifestyle is within your control but *you* lose control. It's natural: forgive yourself and move on. As long as these lapses are few and far between, don't be too rigid with the rules. Being flexible will prevent you from throwing in the towel completely. When you have a setback or fall off the wagon, start the next day with fresh resolve. Slow and steady will keep the fat on one day at a time.

Accessories Just for You

One of the perks of membership in an elite group is customization—special products made with you in mind. With your weight-gain success, you may start needing some of these items:

- **Personal toilet aids:** Whether you choose the Bottom Buddy or Self-Wipe model, these long-handled wipers help you help yourself.

- **Long-handled toe washer:** Provides assistance with the foot's nooks and crannies.

- **No-bend toenail clipper:** Another extended-reach item, activated at knee level by a pistol pull. Some models come with magnifying lens.

- **Dressing aids:** Why bend over when you could get a button hook, zipper pull, or implements to help you put on your socks?

- **Curved shower-curtain rods:** Replace your straight rod with one that pulls the curtain away from your expanding waistline.

- **Athletic gear:** You won't want to try the super-sized bicycle seat because that activity burns precious calories. However, the Kool Tee Golf Tool allows you to insert and replace tees into the green without bending over.

- **Travel:** Fly in style, security, and comfort with your very own seat belt extender!

Try New Strategies

Falling off the wagon poses one kind of problem, but hitting a plateau is a different matter. If you've been gaining steadily but suddenly your progress halts, perhaps you've reached your maximum fat potential with your current tools. A quick fix would be to slow your metabolism down by skipping breakfast for a week and bingeing in the afternoons. If that doesn't work, review previous chapters and highlight advice you've yet to implement.

Re-reading this book is one antidote for hitting the proverbial wall. If the scale is stalled or spiraling downward and you don't think you can eat another bite, try mixing things up. Maybe unconscious eating worked wonders for you but you never gave emotional eating a fair shake. Is it possible that instead of creating a fat-friendly home environment, you've relied too heavily on takeout? Reviewing these lessons will turn you on to new tools for success and inspire you to resume your fat journey.

Scout's Law

When all else fails, be prepared. Fatty foods with high-fructose corn syrup should be properly stocked in your house, your car, and your workplace. Know the location of convenience stores, takeout restaurants, and bakeries. Bring your own food to parties if you suspect the host will offer lighter fare than you require. The right food won't always appear in front of you at the right time: at the end of the day, you provide for yourself.

Fat Is the Future

Getting fat has done more than just add rolls to your waist, thickness to your thighs, chins to your face, and bulge to your belly. Being obese grants you entrance onto the world stage: you're joining millions of people who celebrate their lives through size.

Recognizing a spectacular and historic change in humanity, the World Health Organization (WHO) has tracked the rise of global obesity. The number of obese people in the world has risen dramatically over the last 10 years, ballooning from 200 million in 1995 to 400 million in 2005. WHO researchers calculate that there are 1.6 billion

Words of Plenty

"Ask not what you can do for your country. Ask what's for lunch."

—Orson Welles

overweight adults in the world. By 2015, WHO predicts that the global tally of overweight success stories will rise to 2.3 billion—including 700 million who are obese!

Fat is the future—first in the United States, and now all over the world. You're finally a part of it! You harnessed your motivation and adopted the right fat-itude. You calibrated your former weight and set attainable goals. You fostered a food-friendly environment, maximized your natural eating instincts, and implemented habits that packed on the pounds. You know what to eat, when to eat it, where to get it, and how much to consume. You have stopped moving. And what was the result? You gained and gained and gained!

Now that you're part of a global phenomenon, it's in your hands to keep your lifelong membership. Fat is the future, so open wide!